Music Brings My Heart Back Home

Music Brings My Heart Back Home

Deanna Edwards

Shadow Mountain
Salt Lake City, Utah

Lyrics to songs written by Deanna Edwards used by permission of Rock Canyon Music Publishers, 777 E. Walnut, Provo, Utah.

Printed in the United States of America

Shadow Mountain is an imprint of Deseret Book Company

First printing March 1988
Second printing July 1988

Library of Congress Cataloging-in-Publication Data

Edwards, Deanna.
Music brings my heart back home.

Includes index.
1. Edwards, Deanna. 2. Music therapists—United States—Biography. 3. Music therapy—United States.
I. Title.
ML429.E356A3 1988 615.8'5154'0924 [B] 87-38123
ISBN 0-87579-112-3

To Dad
whose dying
taught me of living

He never had a dime to spare, his suit was faded gray.
The only things he cared to own were those he gave away.
We used to drive in Dad's old car and talk of things to be,
And I still recall a question my Daddy asked of me.

Where have all the dreamers gone? When did hope get lost?
Sometimes we have to take a risk and never count the cost.
And though our dreams may not come true as our curtain starts to fall,
I'd rather have a broken dream than never dream at all.

The years have passed and Dad's old car has finally turned to rust.
His poems that lay unfinished have crumbled into dust.
But I have a dream to change the world, and sing love's legacy.
My Daddy was a dreamer, and he gave this dream to me!

Contents

Acknowledgments

I am truly grateful for the many people who have woven their colors into the fabric of my life and onto the pages of this book. Specifically, I would like to express thanks—

To my mentors, Elisabeth, Kelly, Joan, and Doug, who planted the seeds.

To my wonderful family, Cliff, Shon, Steve, Jeff, and Eric, who provided the lifegiving rain and sunlight that allowed the seeds to grow.

To my mother, whose love and hard work brought us through the difficult years, and to my special brothers and sisters, who were always there with support and encouragement.

To my friend Shirley Hoffman, who never gave up, and to President Joseph R. Larsen, whose affirmation enlightens us now as it did then.

To the Franciscan Communications Center in Los Angeles, the Christophers in New York, and Dr. Paul Rosene, for believing that music has a far greater mission than has yet been realized.

To the American Health Care Association, the American Nurses Association, and all the organizations that have extended opportunities to share the concepts of music therapy with the helping professions in the United States.

To Bert Chipman, president of the New Brunswick Pastoral Institute, and the Reverend Dermot Buchanan, National

Chaplains adviser in New Zealand, for opening so many doors in Canada and New Zealand.

To my editor, Kerril Sue Rollins, for the tremendous heart work as well as hard work that went into this manuscript. And to Eleanor Knowles for her faith in our message as well as her refinements in the editing process, and Roger Chapman for invaluable help in the final process of proofreading.

To Glen Edwards, who did the beautiful illustrations, and Kent Ware, who designed the book.

To Rick Bingham, Merrill Jenson, and Kenny Hodges, who are responsible for the production of the tape, *Music Brings My Heart Back Home,* which is a companion to this book.

To all the friends whose love and faith continue to bring me energy: Vickie, Sylvia, Maureen, Jann, Gary, Betty, Mary, Jim, Wanda, Dick, Father David, Sister Augusta, my favorite family in Germany, and Michael Ballam, a star whose light comes from within.

I am also grateful for friends who continue to give love and support in their letters, even when I am unable to answer them all, and for those who have given special permission to reprint their thoughts and poems in this book.

1
Dad

"I love you, Deanna."
"I love you, too, Dad."

The fading rays of the afternoon sun penetrated the worn curtains, entered the quiet room, and settled gently upon my father's silver hair. He lay with his back toward me, his shoulder partially covered by a thin white sheet. He appeared to be asleep, and I paused, hesitating to awaken him.

In that moment Dad's words drifted into my thoughts. I remembered him saying, only weeks before my June wedding, "Honey, I can't come to your wedding reception. I haven't been feeling well. But could you please come to see me after the honeymoon?"

Dad was being cared for by close friends in their small country home. I was happy his bed was near a window so he could look out and watch the parade of dancing leaves and hear the summer sounds. In the grassy yard an oak tree, bending over itself, made me think of a stately old man bowing to bless the earth.

My parents divorced when I was three years old. My Norwegian mother was practical, industrious, and hardworking. Dad was an itinerant dreamer, drifting from dream to dream like an old miner splashing his pan into a thousand sparkling streams. His dreams lay like fool's gold in a rusty pan, glittering with the invitation to keep searching. One of his dreams was to be a writer, and his last gift to me was a faded manuscript he hoped would one day be made into a movie. We often talked about his dreams and what we would do when they all came true. Relatives and friends scoffed at the unlikely prospects of their fulfillment, but I had learned long ago, as an awkward teenager gazing at the stars, that it is better to have a dream that never comes true than never to dream at all.

Until my teens I didn't really understand my father. Perhaps that is what made my early walks with him slightly uncomfortable. There was a sense of unreality about our visits. Sometimes they were marred by my wondering if I would be heir to my mother's anger and, yes, outrage, where my father was concerned. She often said he didn't recognize the value of practical responsibilities that could have helped him achieve a successful career. He never met the financial obligations of fatherhood. He was never there to bandage a finger or soothe the hurt when I was rejected by a playmate. He never had enough money to buy himself a suit, much less a new dress for me, and sometimes his clothes looked as if they had been worn forever.

There were times when his futile attempts to give material gifts backfired. Mother once returned a pair of long-wished-for roller skates he had sent me in a shoe box wrapped in brown paper. "These skates are not good enough," she explained as I looked up at her through my tears. "They'll fall apart before long."

In spite of it all, the scattered days I had spent visiting my father during childhood were filled with charm. Dad always believed the best things in life were free, so we had shared precious hours looking for wild daisies and Indian paintbrush on mountain trails. Together we devoured fried chicken and fresh glazed donuts.

When we made our yearly pilgrimage to Bridal Veil Falls in Provo Canyon, it didn't seem to matter that my father was different from most other fathers. Watching the sheets of water smashing down upon the rocks, becoming crystal butterflies, darting up into the sky, I had stopped thinking in terms of "How much did it cost?"

Our happiest hours were those we had spent singing in the car, driving into a fading sunset, or sitting up nights in Dad's old trailer and memorizing songs he had learned as a boy. One song he taught me became a way of life, nudging my frowns into wide-open grins:

Have a smile for everyone you meet
And everyone will have a smile for you.
Every mile along life's busy street
Will lead to friendship true.
Each tomorrow brings new sorrow,
So, why borrow tears?
So, won't you have a smile for everyone you meet
And they will have a smile for you!

As the song lingered in my thoughts, Dad seemed to hear its melody too and began to stir. "Dad," I said in a half-whisper, "the honeymoon was wonderful. We took the station wagon to Yellowstone National Park, and a bear broke into our camp and ate all our food. I missed you at our reception. My wedding dress was so beautiful!"

"Oh, Deanna, I wish I could have been there. I'm so glad you could come."

He turned his face toward me and managed a weak smile. I was so shocked by his appearance that I almost missed his words. In a few short weeks his weight loss had been incredible. He was emaciated and jaundiced; the yellow cast over his face was like the wax of an old, tallow candle. The skin around his lips gathered in wrinkles as if sewn together with invisible thread.

I didn't want Dad to know how upset I was, and I tried hard to blink back the tears burning my eyes. The words forming in my consciousness later became medical terms. "Liver damage." "Mineral imbalance." I needed no physician to spell it out for me. My father was gravely ill. All the love in the world could not change reality: he was dying.

For a few moments I struggled with what to say and

what to do. A part of me wanted to run to him like a little child, bury my face in his thin shoulder, and let my tears fall onto the sheet. "Dad, we've had so little time together. We just have to make the dreams come true. Please live so we can try."

But the adult in me was ever so wary. If I were to follow my feelings and dissolve in tears, Dad would know I knew he was dying. Was he aware of the gravity of his condition? Would my reaction frighten him, depress him, push him further into the dark abyss of illness?

I stood at a crossroads, looking hard at the signs pointing in opposite directions. One read "Honesty and Pain"; the other, "Pretense and Comfort." If I could pretend this wasn't happening, perhaps it wouldn't happen, I thought. Dad would be more comfortable. So would I.

We pursued our silent deception through the long summer as Dad's life ebbed away. We talked about school, about marriage, about the weather, and about everything except the feelings that struggled inside us like frightened children.

Music seemed to ease the fears and fill the hours, so whenever I visited Dad, I brought the guitar I had taught myself to play as a young girl. I sang all the songs we had sung together through the years. The song he seemed to enjoy hearing most was "Whispering Hope." Once, as I sang it, I saw a thinly veiled awareness emerge in his eyes, demanding entrance into my heart. But I couldn't respond to that awareness, and I turned my eyes away.

The last day of September came, and I clung to Dad's presence as the golden leaves clung to the branches of the oak tree outside the window. Afternoon faded into evening, and shadows gathered in the corners of the little farmhouse. But where my father lay, it was bright and beautiful. I didn't know where the light was coming from—perhaps from embers in the western sky, perhaps from my father's soul.

My guitar was leaning against the seat of a chair. I bowed my head as I sat at my father's bedside, groping for the right words to say good-bye to the man who was half the reason for my existence. Mother. Father. Roots digging deeply into my origin. *What would it feel like to be half an orphan?* I wondered.

I felt a warm hand behind my head. Dad pulled my head down onto his chest until his lips rested against my ear. "I love you, Deanna," he whispered.

There was no one else in the room to hear him, even if he had spoken aloud. But his words had penetrated my very soul. There were no more walls between us, no more games to play.

"I love you too, Dad," I said softly. "I love you too."

It was a moment that would live forever in my heart—perhaps the only moment of real truth we had shared during his illness.

A few days later I was standing in my mother-in-law's sunny kitchen, clearing the last remnants of the luncheon dishes from the table, when the telephone rang. It was my brother, calling to tell me Dad had slipped into a coma from which he never awakened and had died quietly in a nearby hospital.

I found myself repressing the feelings that struggled within me, and there were no tears to fill my eyes. I was troubled by their absence and asked myself, "Deanna, did you love your father so little that you can't cry now that he's gone?"

My question was quickly answered by my belief, my faith, that death is not the end, only the beginning of a glorious journey into immortality. I knew instinctively that I would see my father again. I already sensed the presence of his continuing love. Tears seemed an affront to that faith. Still there was an emptiness. I felt like a lonely child sitting in an abandoned schoolroom, yet I knew, strangely enough, that I was also the teacher. Part of me was the inexperienced, awkward schoolteacher, part of me the bewildered student, asking for answers that the teacher could not give—not yet.

I had not been feeling well, and that seemed reason enough for me to decline the opportunity to attend Dad's funeral. The prospect of seeing him lying in a casket was disquieting. I didn't want to remember him that way. I wanted to remember my father in a thousand other life-giving ways—his laughter, his sense of humor, the serious, theological side born of pioneer parents who came to the West for a cause. My favorite picture of Dad could never be captured with a camera. He was standing somewhere against a canvas of autumn leaves, his silver hair painted with sunlight.

The night before the funeral, the memories begged for attention. The teacher in me said Dad would be disappointed if I did not find a way to send part of myself to the funeral. We needed to share the love and loss together. I gathered pen and paper together and wrote a tribute to a man who had long known the meaning of rejection. It was my last act of acceptance of all that he was.

My husband, Cliff, promised to share at the funeral service what I tried to capture of my father's life on those scraps of paper:

He loved to live life's moments dear,
To drink the sage-filled mountain air,
And show me fields of flowers fair—
This much of him I know.

He loved the roses in the dawn,
A mountain trail to walk upon,
Or sun's bright warmth when night was gone—
This side of him I know!

He loved to sing,
And when life's happy moments fell
Like sunbeams in a pleasant vale,
Or when life's darker moments came
And twilight singled out the stars,
He sang to me remembered songs of long ago.

When autumn's crisp brought winter's breeze
And frost that painted all the trees,
Dropped leaves that fell like memories,
He loved them all.

I do not feel that he is gone—
Just hidden in the far beyond
Like stars that vanish in the dawn.

For he believed so strongly then
That life goes on. He lives again!
He walks in autumn's sunny glen
And sings the songs that we sang then!
This much of him I know!

2

Volunteer with a Guitar

It had been nine years since my father's death, and sometimes I felt a twinge of resentment that our sons would never sit on their grandfather's lap and see the creases deepen around his eyes when he laughed, or hear his robust voice burst into a song. How Dad would have loved them! I knew he must be watching his grandsons from somewhere. If only heaven were not so far away.

A job offer for my husband from Illinois State University had lured us to the Midwest, and I was learning to appreciate the rich and fertile farmlands surrounding us in Normal, Illinois. But mountain memories still tugged at my heart. Perhaps it wouldn't be so difficult to be twelve hundred miles from home, I sometimes thought, if we could sit in Grandma's kitchen on an occasional Sunday afternoon and consume one of her homemade chocolate cakes, or take our little sons to play with their cousins. Because of the great distance separating us, we were limited to one summer visit home each year, phone calls, and letters.

I forced my thoughts away from yesterdays and began reviewing my morning tasks. A jangling telephone suddenly interrupted my plans. I recognized Shirley Hoffman's voice on the other end.

Shirley was always involved in one project or another. How she found time to be wife, mother, president of the women's auxiliary of our church, and president of the hospital auxiliary, I could never figure out. I knew instinctively why she was calling and could have said the words right along with her. "Deanna, I'm going to be doing some volunteer work at the hospital tomorrow. Would you care to come with me?"

She had extended the invitation many times, and every time I had said, "No!" Sometimes my refusals had dissolved into teasing comments: "Shirley, someday when I'm old and gray I'll come to the hospital and help the auxiliary make quilts." On the other days I had a Sunday School lesson to prepare or a house to clean. I couldn't figure out why she hadn't given up on me long ago. In any case, my ready supply of excuses was dwindling. Then I thought of Jeff. "What about Jeff?" I asked. "He's not in school yet, and it would be difficult at this late hour to find a baby-sitter."

Shirley was more than delighted to provide me with an instant solution. "Mennonite Hospital has a fantastic nursery, and they care for the children of volunteers free of charge. They even serve free meals to volunteers in the cafeteria." She paused for a moment, testing the silence, then added, "This could be an excellent opportunity for Jeff to make new friends."

It occurred to me that the best way to put an end to Shirley's incessant pressure would be to join her, but my commitment had to be qualified. "All right," I said reluctantly, "I'll come and do some volunteer work at the hospital, but I can only stay for half a day. I'm not sure how I could be of help, but it deserves at least a try."

I could feel the smile in Shirley's voice. "You'll need to have an interview with Rachael, our volunteer supervisor, as soon as you arrive at the hospital in the morning. She'll give you a brief orientation, and you can let her know if there's a specific area of the hospital where you'd like to work." She paused, and her voice softened. "Deanna, I'm glad you're going to come tomorrow. My life has changed in so many ways since I started working there. I've had a feeling for a long time that there's a special work waiting for you."

The remainder of the day I found myself resisting the

idea of going to the hospital for half a day. I was chagrined at the thought of going through a formal interview with the volunteer supervisor for just a few hours' work. Gradually I became aware that lack of time was not the only factor in my reluctance to become a volunteer. Hospitals had always been formidable places for me, with their somber, sterile atmosphere, strict visiting hours, uniformed nurses and doctors hurrying about with formal purpose, and "Quiet Please" signs in the corridors. A part of me was drawn to television shows about hospitals, but beyond that fascination, some quiet, unnamed fear was responsible for my earlier refusals. Was it fear of failure? fear of rejection? fear of the unknown? Whatever it was, fear would have to wait. At least, I thought with relief, I would only have to worry about it for half a day.

Mennonite Hospital was located in Bloomington, a twin city to our little town of Normal. I felt both shy and scared as I took the elevator to the lower level and walked down the long hallway leading to the Department of Volunteers.

Rachael was a pleasant woman with silver-gray hair piled on top of her head. She greeted me with a motherly smile and a warm handshake. Her name tag was pinned to the left collar of her coral pink jacket, the standard uniform for volunteers in the hospital. She ushered me into a small, tidy office and handed me a form to fill out. As I wrote down "art, creative writing, and music" on the line requesting special interests and hobbies, I wondered how those could provide any special qualifications for hospital work. I was still filling out the form when Rachael asked me a question. "Deanna, why do you want to be a volunteer?" she pointedly asked, catching me off guard.

What could I say? That I had come only to appease a persistent friend? I hardly remember my response, but the question brought my motives and fears sharply into focus. I didn't have the heart to tell her I would be staying only half a day.

Rachael explained that volunteer programs supplement

the duties of the regular hospital staff by rendering services that would not otherwise be possible. "Furthermore," she added, "volunteers enhance the public image of the hospital and help with vital fund-raising projects."

She handed me a little card that listed qualifications desired for hospital volunteers: personal integrity, physical fitness, emotional stability, loyalty to the institution, and reliability. Service areas included the gift and library carts; the feeding of incapacitated patients; mail delivery; assistance in physical therapy, activity therapy, and surgery; shampoo service; and hostess activities. I already knew which area I would request, remembering my favorite television shows. If I worked in emergency, I reasoned, maybe I could help rescue the patients coming in, just as they did on television. Never mind that I'd never had a first-aid or CPR class.

"Would it be all right if I worked in emergency or surgery this morning?" I asked cautiously.

Rachael was scanning the sheet I had filled out. She laid it on the desk, her eyes meeting mine. "After reading through this list of things you like to do, I believe you would be happier working in the Activity Therapy Department," she said with firm, professional warmth. "Mennonite Hospital is divided into two units. Basically, it's a general hospital and nursing home combined. Special activities are provided mostly for residents in our long-term care unit. Vickie Lannie is the nurse in charge of that department and will tell you more about your duties."

She handed me a booklet on volunteer work and asked me to read it in my spare time. "I'm so happy you've decided to join us," she said.

Moments later I was standing in the doorway of a brightly lit room. The nurse in charge of the Activity Therapy Department had stepped out briefly to run an errand, and I carefully surveyed the scene before me. Posters almost hid three of the cream-colored walls, and large shelves stretched from floor to ceiling against the other wall. Stuffed animals peered out at me from the shelves, and octopuses made of yarn dangled long legs over the sides. Half-painted ceramic figurines stood beside partially filled jars of paint, waiting to be finished.

In the center of the room, some elderly people sat around a large table cutting nylons into small pieces. A woman in a pink sweater dipped her hand into a huge box of nylons, brought out a fistful, and placed them in the center of the table. "We'll have to cut a lot of nylons to stuff all these pillows in time for the bazaar," she said.

My dreams of heroism faded as I contemplated four hours of nylon cutting. I thought of the phrase I often used when I went into the dentist's office: "This too shall pass."

Discovering an extra pair of scissors lying on a nearby desk, I squeezed into a vacant chair between two of the residents. *In four hours I'll be free again,* I said to myself.

On my left was a delicate, elderly woman wearing a pink bed jacket. On my right sat an elderly man who introduced himself as Ira Thomas. He reminded me of an ancient tree with long trunk and gnarled limbs. I noticed first his hands, the wrinkles forming miniature canyons and valleys. They were so big that he could hardly lock them around the small scissors he was holding. His eyebrows hung low over dramatic blue eyes that suddenly caught mine. Even more penetrating than his eyes was the fire burning within them.

"Are you our new volunteer?" he asked.

I wanted to say, "Only for half a day," but I just nodded my head slightly.

"Would you like to hear some of my poetry?" he asked.

I had never before heard the many poems he had memorized. No doubt the residents around the table had heard them countless times. He shared them with me one by one, poems about old farms and childhood sweethearts, about slow summer days and sailing ships. Suddenly the flame leaped in his eyes, and he looked searchingly at me as though wondering if he could trust me with one of the deepest secrets of his life. "Have you ever heard the poem called 'The Shooting of Dan McGrew'?" he asked in a hushed voice.

I had to admit that I had not.

"I learned that poem when I was a kid," he said, "and I guarantee you that was many, many years ago."

Never before had a story come so alive for me than on that day as I listened to old Ira. I felt as though I were actually there, in the Malamute Saloon in the dim light of some forgotten yesterday. Dangerous Dan McGrew was playing a solo game of cards in the corner under the watchful eye of "the lady known as Lou." A miner, fresh from the creek, stumbled in, spotted the old piano, and went over and covered the keys with hands that must have looked just like Ira's. I stopped cutting nylons so I could watch the animated gestures and the expressions on Ira's face. As his voice trembled with emotion, I had the strong feeling he had lived that poem:

> Were you ever out in the Great Alone,
> When the moon was awful clear,
> And the icy mountains hemmed you in
> With a silence you most could hear;
> With only the howl of the timber wolf,
> And you camped there in the cold,
> A half-dead thing in a stark, dead world,
> Clean mad for the muck called gold;
> While high overhead, green, yellow and red,
> The North Lights swept in bars?—
> Then you've a haunch what the music meant . . .
> Hunger and night and the stars.

Suddenly Ira seemed to be speaking over a big lump that had formed deep inside, and tears welled in his eyes. He was determined to allow his long-kept secret to fall out of the poem, hoping it would be caught by a gentle heart. He cleared his throat with much effort and uttered words that seemed to come from the depths of his soul:

> And hunger not of the belly kind,
> That's banished with bacon and beans,
> But the gnawing hunger of a lonely man
> For a home and all that it means.

It hit my heart with a thud. The "secret" was his hunger

for home! I had been complaining about spending four hours away from my home, and it was quite possible that Ira Thomas would never go home again. He had shared his deepest need with a total stranger! His incredible yearning made my soul ache for him. After pulling together his emotions, he continued, haltingly:

> For the fireside far from the cares that are,
> Four walls and a roof above;
> But oh, so crammful of cosy joy,
> And crowned with a woman's love.*

As Ira finished the poem, he laid his scissors on the table and turned to me, the glimmer of a smile on his lips. "I had the privilege of having two of the finest women that ever lived," he said.

"Oh, you were married twice?" I asked, finding myself deeply interested in his story.

"Yes, and both of 'em passed on."

"I'm sorry," I said softly. "You must get lonesome sometimes."

"Oh, you bet I do!" he exclaimed. Several other residents glanced up from their work. "I was twenty-one years between marriages and had three children by my first wife. I never had enough money to ask a girl to have a stick of chewing gum, much less dinner, until all my kids were through college. Then I married again. My advice to anybody who loses their mate is to hurry and find another one, because it's terrible to live alone."

For a moment the room was quiet. The lady in the pink jacket nodded in agreement, for Ira's words echoed the thoughts and longings of the others who sat with us at the table. Then his voice changed, and conviction, edged with hope, brightened his words. He looked up, beyond the narrow confines of the activity therapy room, into a shining possibility. "I believe, even with all my afflictions right now,

*Robert Service, "The Shooting of Dan McGrew," *The Spell of the Yukon* (New York: Dodd, Mead & Co., 1963), p. 55.

that I'm going to get well. I'll be glad when this day here is just a memory and I'm back home and able to take care of myself."

I knew that Ira would probably never return to his own home again, but his was the hope that maintains life. Much of that hope centered on his children, whom he obviously loved deeply.

"I've got a boy who comes almost every day and a daughter who's been here several times from Florida," he told me. "I'm sure I'd have been dead if it hadn't been for those kids. I can't say too much about my wives and my three children. They've been the greatest blessings, outside my mother, that God could ever give to one man."

"Love keeps you alive, doesn't it," I said, only beginning to realize the true meaning of those words.

"You bet it does!" Ira responded with conviction. "But you have to remember, nobody is ever alone. God is with you every moment of the day and night. The important thing is to remember to trust Him. When I was a little kid, my mother once told me that if you get up in the morning and there's an empty plate staring you in the face, you weren't to worry. 'Before the day is over,' she'd say, 'God will give you food.' "

Ira's head bowed once more over his task, his smooth, bare crown reflecting the light above us. "I see a lot of lonely people here in the hospital that I feel sorry for. They don't have anybody who ever comes to see them."

Without hesitation, a timid voice spoke up in the room. "Ira, if you have a friend that nobody comes to see, please let me know, and I will come."

I was startled to realize that the voice was mine! It was my first commitment to care for someone outside my safe, private world of family and friends. It was a commitment that would change my life. I repeated the words silently to myself, *Please let me know, and I will come*. At last, love had become greater than fear.

A dark-haired woman with a radiant face bounced into

the room. "I'm back, everyone," she said cheerfully. Then she noticed me.

"I'm Vickie Lannie, the nurse in charge of the Activity Therapy Department," she said, smiling. "I see you took good care of my residents while I was running an errand. Rachael told me you're our new volunteer. She said that on the form you filled out, you mentioned a special interest in music. Do you sing?"

"Yes," I admitted. "I love to sing, and sometimes I perform for local groups."

"Aha! A kindred spirit! Our residents just love music!" she exclaimed. "Would you mind singing a few songs for them?"

Ira Thomas raised his head and squinted at me. "Do you happen to know the song 'Among My Souvenirs'?"

"Of course," I responded. "My father taught me that song years ago."

As I began to sing, Ira joined in with unmistakable enthusiasm. His voice filled the room with strength and clarity.

I had not sung the old song for years, but slowly it and Dad's other favorites came drifting into my consciousness—"Let Me Call You Sweetheart," "Yours," "Just a Cottage Small by a Waterfall."

Soon the other residents were singing too. Smiles were returning and toes were tapping as they recalled and shared memories.

After the residents had returned to their rooms, Vickie and I discussed the success of our impromptu sing-along. The purpose of the Activity Therapy Department, Vickie explained, was to provide meaningful activities for long-term care residents, to teach them new skills, and to help them feel the satisfaction of personal accomplishment. Activities were also intended to keep their bodies and spirits active, encouraging social integration through group activities.

"Music is a good way to bring people together," Vickie explained. "When I was in nurse's training, I used to bring my guitar in and sing to my patients. I learned that music is

much more than entertainment. It is therapy as well. Music allows a patient to relate to a nurse in a special way, and it opens lines of communication that might not be open otherwise. Perhaps your musical experience and ability will give us a chance to use music more in our department as well as other areas of the hospital. When you come back next Thursday, would you mind bringing your guitar? Perhaps we can sing in some of the patients' rooms." Vickie wasn't yet aware of my previous half-hearted commitment.

The words "next Thursday" jumped out at me. My plan

to volunteer for only half a day dissolved in my anticipation of seeing Vickie and Ira again. What a wonderful idea—to sing to the patients! I had never heard of music therapy, but it sounded like a subject I wanted to learn more about. Ever since I had sung at my dying father's bedside, I had wanted to use my music abilities for more than entertainment. I wanted to touch people, to teach them, to motivate them with music. Mennonite Hospital could be the perfect setting for such a learning experience to begin.

"Of course I'll bring my guitar," I said. "I'll be here shortly before nine o'clock next Thursday morning." I was beginning to look upon my next visit as an exciting adventure.

When I walked out of the hospital, I felt as if I were walking on air. I had entered the hospital for all the wrong reasons, but I would be returning for all the right ones. I could hardly wait for next Thursday to come.

After dinner that evening, I talked nonstop to my husband about my day. Then he said, "I'd be proud to have you share your time and talents with patients in the hospital. I can't think of anyone who needs love and attention more than they do. Just be sure you share your adventures with me."

I showed him the booklet Rachael had given me that morning. Together we read a prayer at the end of it:

> Almighty God and Heavenly Father of Mankind, bless, we pray Thee, our endeavors in those hospitals in which we strive to bring comfort and hope to all who are in distress of mind or body.
>
> Guide us so that we may use the privilege given us to help the aged, the ill and the very young with generosity, with discretion and with gentleness. Give us the strength to labor diligently, the courage to think and to speak with clarity and conviction but without prejudice or pride.
>
> Grant us, we beseech Thee, both wisdom and humility in directing our united efforts to do for others only as Thou would have us do. Amen.

3

Music: A Language of Love

The following Thursday, while Vickie and I were taking a tour of the hospital, she explained the purposes of each area—the medical, surgical, eye care, physical therapy, and long-term care units. Nurses in crisp uniforms bustled about the nurses' stations, and now and then a volunteer, pushing a cart or carrying a vase of flowers, disappeared into a patient's room. We passed the intensive-care unit and a room filled with anxiously waiting family members. The concerned expression on each face revealed an untold story, an unspoken prayer.

"We have such a wide variety of patients here. You'll discover that needs and emotions vary over a broad spectrum," Vickie explained. "Many residents in the long-term care unit have been here for months, some for years. Patients in short-term care are here to be treated for severe illnesses and injuries. Others are here to undergo minor or major surgery, and many are frightened and uncertain. And some," she added, "are unable to communicate at all. Some have suffered a stroke or brain damage. A few are comatose and appear to be unaware of what's happening around them. In the case of those with a fatal injury or a terminal illness, hearing is often the last of the senses to go. We must not neglect these patients when we sing on the units. In any kind of patient care, we must never assume that a person can't hear just because there is no response."

Vickie stressed the importance of volunteers working in

concert with other staff members and sharing our findings with them. She'd had considerable experience working with patients in all areas of care, and I found her to be both a comfort and a source of education. Her wonderful sense of humor was evident even in the presence of serious professionalism. She was warm, amusing, and sensitive—qualities that put me at ease as I pulled together the fragile threads of my own self-confidence and prepared to enter a patient's room for the first time.

Vickie had received permission to devote time on Thursdays to a music program for patients in areas of the hospital outside the Activity Therapy Department. We decided to begin each week in the eye-care unit and proceed to other floors in a predictable pattern so staff members would know approximately when to expect us.

"Our patients have a great need for privacy," Vickie explained. "So much of their individual identity is stripped from them when they enter a hospital setting. The concept of using music in a general hospital is new. Entering a patient's room is an invasion of privacy, and we must be certain that our intrusion is a pleasant one."

Gradually I realized that we were, in a very real sense, pioneering. We were not experienced in the use of music in a therapeutic setting, nor did we have enough information to give us answers to our numerous questions. But we both had enthusiasm and the expertise to communicate with patients through music, and we were aware that experience would be our teacher.

Experience would teach me that music is a language of love and release. It intensifies, reminds, beautifies, teaches, saddens, gladdens, enlivens, and pervades all human life. Music can help unite a family, heal a broken heart, inspire an indigent spirit.

"When we introduce ourselves to the patients," Vickie said, "we must be sure we have permission to enter their rooms. They must be given the freedom to choose whether to share the musical experience with us. We must not intimidate them or make them feel they must listen to us."

We walked through the eye-care unit and stopped at the last door. Butterflies fluttered in my stomach as I peered into the semidarkness of the room of our first patient. I was relieved when Vickie initiated the introduction.

"Hello, I'm Vickie Lannie, and I'm a nurse here," she began. "Deanna is a volunteer. We're wondering if it would be all right if we came in to sing a few songs for you."

"Please come in," came a soft voice from the darkness. "I'd appreciate a song so much."

I was filled with a sense of awe and mystery upon entering the room. The man lying in the bed appeared to be in his thirties. His long face and sharp features were accentuated by thick brown hair. Patches covered his eyes.

"I've been lying here thinking," he said. "Sometimes it's not good to think too much—especially now. I'm going to have surgery tomorrow, and that's all I think about. The television isn't much good—can't see it anyway. A song would be a welcome diversion for me right now."

He gestured toward a small, cluttered nightstand by his bed. A vase of carnations partially covered the photo of a young woman, her arm gently embracing a small child. "You don't realize how beautiful your loved ones are until you can't see them anymore."

We pulled two chairs close beside his bed. Then I asked, "What kind of music do you like?" I had a file at home filled with songs I had learned through the years from almost every category of music. I played by ear and needed only to save the words, most of which I had committed to memory.

"I've always been a country-music fan," he said. "But I like gospel music too."

Vickie and I had already compared notes on the songs we both knew and could sing together. For this patient we chose "Just a Closer Walk with Thee," harmonizing quickly and easily, and then blended our voices on a short medley of familiar tunes. Next, Vickie sang a humorous song that was to become one of our favorites, and laughter soon filled the room.

"I can almost see you in my mind," the patient said, "especially when you laugh. Those of us who have trouble with our eyes develop a sense about people. We can 'hear' what you look like. And you both 'sound' like good friends to me."

"To quote the words of an old song, 'A stranger's just a friend you do not know,' " I said, finding myself reluctant to leave the room. "Before we go, there's a gospel song that Vickie and I both love. It's called 'He Touched Me.' We're still pretty new at this and we haven't practiced much, but we hope you like it."

I was impressed with the sweet quality of Vickie's voice, her clarity of sound, and her wide vocal range. I picked up an easy alto harmony as she sang the melody. Faith touched the darkness with its brilliance as we finished with the words: "He touched me and made me whole." While we were getting ready to leave, the patient reached out and caught my arm with his hand. "The surgery I'm going to have tomorrow may restore my sight, but there's also a chance the operation will fail. Your music has given me the courage I need to face possible blindness."

We walked into the hallway, and I realized that I was more aware of the gift of sight than I had ever been before. "Vickie," I said, blinking back tears, "I didn't know it would be like this. What if I should start to cry—right in front of a patient?"

"What would be so terrible about that?" she asked. "Sometimes the best gift you can give patients is to cry with them."

As we worked our way from room to room, moving closer to the nurses' station, we noticed a nurse doing a soft-shoe dance in the hall and another tapping out rhythm on a notebook with a pencil. "We need this music more than the patients do!" a nurse exclaimed with a smile. "You can come back to our floor anytime!"

Only one patient on the unit refused to let us sing. Then he appeared later in the doorway of the room of another patient we were singing to, clutching a bathrobe around his stocky form."I changed my mind," he said gruffly. "I want a song."

On the medical unit, a young woman noticed Vickie and me with our guitars and hurried over to us. "My mother has been in a coma for some time," she said. "I don't know if she'll be able to hear you, but her favorite song is 'In the Garden.' Would you mind going into her room and singing to her? Even if she can't hear you, it would mean so much to me."

She led us to her mother's room. The curtains had been flung wide open, inviting in the sunshine and the hope that the patient might see and feel the glorious light. The woman lay motionless. Vickie reached across the shiny metal bar of the bed and took her hand. I had never even seen a comatose patient, and I said a silent prayer as we prepared to sing.

We sang the first verse and chorus of the song and were just beginning to move into the second verse—"He speaks, and the sound of His voice is so sweet the birds hush their singing"—when the woman began moving her lips, ever so slightly at first. Then she broke into wavering sounds of song: "He walks with me and He talks with me, and He tells me I am His own." We sang the chorus together while the daughter stood at the foot of the bed, tears streaming down her cheeks. When we finished, the patient's eyes fluttered open, and she looked at us searchingly. "How did you know that's my favorite song?" she asked.

Vickie and I wanted to laugh, cry, and hug each other, all at the same time. Somehow the familiar strains of the hymn had done what words alone could not do: it had touched a responsive chord deep within the patient. We reported her response to the nurses' station before returning to the Activity Therapy Department, where we had planned a lunch-hour sing-along with the residents. They enjoyed waving their arms or clapping in rhythm to familiar tunes.

While I played the guitar and led the singing, Vickie led them in exercises, sometimes pausing beside their chairs to help them keep time with the rhythm.

Before I left, Vickie and I discussed our experiences with the patients we had sung to that morning. "In the very sick or elderly, the desire to act, to plan, to achieve is very low," she explained. "We try to help them experience what it means to *do* things, to show them they are indeed capable of reaching a goal. Progress must have a beginning. Sometimes a stroke patient who hasn't responded to other therapeutic techniques can smile and keep time with music. A song might help others to feel free to tell you their fears. Once patients realize they can perform a given task, even the simple task of singing or keeping time, then they are ready for the next, more difficult step."

"Vickie, there are so many patients we didn't have a chance to sing for today," I said. "I don't think a half day will be enough. If you can get some extra help in the Activity Therapy Department, do you suppose we could work full days on Thursdays? I don't think my family would mind."

As I spoke, I sensed a new and deep fulfillment coming into my life. My thoughts of self-concern were turning to the physical and emotional well-being of others. My half day a week was begging to become a way of life. I was beginning to learn the language of love.

It is often said that hospitals are bastions of sterility and rigid tradition, but Mennonite Hospital definitely did not fit the stereotype. Its warm, caring atmosphere made it easier for Vickie and me to venture into the hallways each Thursday with our guitars.

We quickly became aware of the unique stimulative and sedative qualities of songs. We used fast, up-tempo tunes with the residents during their exercise sessions and found that stroke victims were able to move their bodies more easily to music. Even if it was just a toe moving in rhythm under the sheet, it was exciting to witness that response. Those who had suffered speech impairment because of brain damage, stroke, or drug overdose would often attempt to hum or sing along with us, and I discovered that their speech rehabilitation was facilitated through the use of music.

Slower, more mellow music helped patients relax and let go of fears and anxieties. Whenever we sang in the intensive-care unit, we chose only quiet, soothing songs, singing to the patients on a one-to-one basis. Alleviation of fear and pain was most often the result.

After introducing ourselves to the patients, we would ask what kind of music they liked, and we avoided the question, "What is your favorite song?" We didn't want to put anyone on the spot or have to apologize for not knowing any favorites. We named categories such as country, pop, religious, folk, or classical. Giving patients a choice often led them to give a personal prescription that reflected their needs and feelings at that moment.

In time, as we cultivated our instincts and formulated opinions about our work, we established guidelines for using music in different areas of the hospital. We learned to inquire at the nurses' stations about rooms we should not enter, where patients with recent surgeries or contagious illnesses were resting. We also asked if certain patients might benefit from a song.

I found the work so fascinating that I began to keep a journal, recording my observations on the effect of music in patient care. Our music program captured the attention of the local media, and soon newspapers in Illinois and Utah carried stories about our efforts, including the patient who had been in a coma and had responded so amazingly. We began to receive letters from people who had experienced firsthand what it was like to be comatose.

Paralytic encephalitis had cut off Jean Whittaker's ability to move, she wrote me. She was unable to speak or communicate in any way. When staff or family members came into her hospital room, they spoke around her and to each other but never directly to her. She described the sensation of being in a small, thin, black box—small because she couldn't move, black because she couldn't see, and thin because she heard everything. She was unable to move, talk, or see, and wanted to cry out, "I'm here! Please know I'm here!"

Two nurses helped give Jean the strength to get through her experience. One would hum or sing inspirational songs whenever she was in the room. This gave Jean a tremendous lift because even though words were not being said, there was vital communication through music. She looked forward to one day meeting the nurse, who Jean thought must be very beautiful.

The other nurse talked about normal, everyday things—the sight of snow on the branches of trees as she drove to work or news about local and national events. "It was a way for me to see images in my mind," Jean explained, "a way for me to get out of my prison and keep in touch with life."

After surviving the experience, Jean wanted to go through the hospital and tell everyone to communicate with those who were comatose and others who were unable to respond. I promised I would help to spread that message and would encourage nurses to use music with patients, even if it only came from a tape recorder placed by the patient's bedside. We decided, with a chuckle, that a tape recorder was best. If a radio was left on unattended by a patient's bedside, the patient might stay in a coma just to get away from the music! What mattered was that patients hear music they loved when they were well.

In another letter, Andrew Cackling, from a small Illinois town, said this:

> Dear Mrs. Edwards,
>
> Nine years ago I had five very serious heart attacks and spent thirty-one days in the hospital as a result. I learned several lessons in the process of getting back on my feet again, but one lesson has left a very deep impression on me. I had always felt—and had told my family so—that we should never say anything inappropriate in the presence of someone who was in a coma or who seemed to be asleep, and I found out that this is true. Many times I could hear what was going on around me and could not let people know I could hear. I was lucky that my family and my doctor did not talk about my condition in my room. But sometimes if a patient who starts to get well acts strange with certain people, it is perhaps because of some thoughtless conversation he has overheard. I hope this letter will help someone else.

As I read these letters, I became more aware that comatose patients are often completely isolated from sounds and communication and that friends and staff members sometimes make thoughtless remarks, assuming they won't be heard. I thought of a comment made by a nurse in one of the rooms I was visiting: "I think this patient has lost the will to live and will probably die soon." If the patient heard her, I worried, it could hasten her prediction. Fortunately, most people in the helping professions are increasingly aware of the patient's ability to hear and of the need for warm and sensitive conversation with unresponsive patients, even though a one-sided verbal exchange is not always easy. I have also seen tears on the cheeks of those who are unable to respond.

The administrator of Mennonite Hospital, Bill Dunn, had been supportive of our music program from the beginning, but when I met him in the hallway one day, a slow smile crossed his lips and he said, "Try to bring your program in through *evolution* and not *revolution!*"

Not everyone felt that music had a therapeutic effect on patients. When I shared my excitement about the possibilities of music as therapy with an assistant administrator in the hospital, he exclaimed, "Wait a minute! Let's not make this more than it is! It's wonderful that you can come and sing to our patients, but music is entertainment, not therapy. What's therapeutic about patients smiling or tapping their toes to music? I know that patients love music, but I wonder if you could name ten things about it that are therapeutic."

His comments frustrated me, but at the same time they challenged me. Shortly afterwards I called the music department at Illinois State University and was soon talking with the department chairman, Dr. Paul Rosene. A dynamic instructor, he expressed a strong interest in our program at the hospital and a deep appreciation for it.

"You won't believe this," Dr. Rosene said, "but we have a brand new music therapy department at our university. It has been a dream of mine for many years, and we're very proud to be one of the few universities in our state to have such a department. Never let anyone tell you that music is just entertainment. I would appreciate it if you could share a little about your music program with my students, and afterward we can meet in my office and I'll tell you about what we're doing here at the university to promote music therapy."

It was refreshing to meet a kindred spirit. I promptly enrolled as a part-time music therapy student and began to learn how much I didn't know. In addition to our theoretical studies, we were given opportunities to put theory and practice together.

I learned that music therapy involves effecting a change in the physical, mental, spiritual, and emotional well-being of a patient through music, and that those who achieve a degree in this field are called registered music therapists. Illinois State University was one of a growing number of schools throughout the nation offering a music therapy program.

We students were given opportunities to work with children with Down's Syndrome, with emotionally disturbed young people, and with physically and mentally handicapped children and adults. I found it fascinating to go to such institutions as the Lincoln State School in Lincoln, Illinois, to observe other music therapists at work.

The objective in many of the schools we visited is to use music as therapy and a teaching tool to help handicapped children function better in other areas of their lives—to teach them about emotions, their bodies, academic subjects, and ways to function normally. If a child can learn to pick up a stick and beat a drum, why can't he learn to pick up a spoon and feed himself, or to tie his shoes? The possibilities are limitless!

Many registered music therapists we observed work to a large extent with group activities, but I found that the one-to-one relationship with a resident or a patient is also rewarding. It became my favorite way of relating to patients. Children who cannot see often develop highly refined skills in music, and those who are deaf can learn to feel the rhythms by placing their hands on a drum or a guitar as it is being played.

Prior to 1944, no formal training existed for those interested in music therapy, even though the concept was as old as the beginning of man. Many primitive civilizations put music and medicine together for healing purposes. During World War II, dedicated American Red Cross volunteers pushed pianos around the wards of veterans' hospitals to bring music to the patients.

Those who know of E. Thayer Gaston's exceptional work

in this field fondly call him "the father of music therapy" because of his untiring efforts to see that music was recognized by the American Medical Association as valid therapy. When the AMA recognized music as a therapy in 1950, programs began to spring up in universities and colleges around the nation, leading to many new books and research projects in the field. Gaston co-authored and edited the pioneering book *Music in Therapy.*

Even though I could not function as a registered therapist until I earned a degree, I could continue to use music in a therapeutic way as a volunteer. I discovered early in my work that many patients love to sing and, when given the freedom to do so, find emotional release and great satisfaction.

One afternoon when Vickie and I passed the nurses' station on the surgical unit, we noticed a physician looking over a patient's chart. Timidly I said, "Well, here we are, doctor, making noise again."

The doctor, a man of few words, spoke to us without looking up. "Yes, but it's a *joyful* noise!"

What better place to hear a joyful noise than in a hospital? I asked myself.

On the surgical unit we entered the room of Mr. Jones, who lay flat in his bed, tension knitting his bushy eyebrows together. He was a large man with sandy hair and ruddy complexion, but today his face was more pale than usual. At least it seemed so as he lay against the white sheets, his fingers clenched together. Vickie told me Mr. Jones would soon be going in for gallbladder surgery. His manner reminded me of my own mother shortly before her surgery. The thought of undergoing an operation, minor or major, is traumatic for many, as it was for her. The day before she entered the hospital, she called me and asked, "Deanna, is there anything you'd like before I go to the hospital?"

"Not really, Mother," I responded, "except that I'd like you to get well very soon."

She hesitated, then asked, "Isn't there a vase, a favorite picture, something that would be meaningful to you?"

It gradually dawned on me that my mother might be concerned about surviving surgery and wanted to send me something to remember her by. I asked for my favorite picture—one of her as a child, sitting with one of my uncles. Days later the faded picture arrived. Mother went through her surgery well, returned home, and soon recovered. Several months later I received another call. "Deanna, I miss the picture I sent you. Would you mind sending it back, please?"

I smiled as I thought of her anxiety, realizing that Mr. Jones must be feeling very much the same way.

"Do you kids work in this hospital?" he inquired, looking curiously at our guitars.

"I'm a nurse here," Vickie explained.

"I'm just a volunteer," I said.

"What do you mean, 'just a volunteer'?" Vickie demanded. "I feed you, don't I?"

"That's true," I admitted. "She does give me a little treat once in a while."

"It's never a little for her," Vickie said, laughing.

Mr. Jones relaxed and began to chuckle. I leaned closer and said, "I haven't told this to anyone else, but there are only two reasons why I sing to patients in this hospital. No matter how bad I sound, my audience can't get up and walk out on me, and sometimes the patients give me free chocolates."

I could tell by the look on Mr. Jones's face that I'd won his heart. "I love 'em too," he confided. "I hate to tell you this, but I don't have any chocolates right now. But they're going to take out my gallbladder tomorrow, and I sure could use a good song."

"Is there a special kind of music you like?" I asked.

"You bet," he said. "I love to sing those old southern gospel hymns. They sure don't write 'em like they used to!" He hesitated a moment, then requested a most appropriate song for the occasion. "Do you happen to know 'When the Roll Is Called Up Yonder I'll Be There'?"

In a flash I read his thoughts. He was afraid he just might

". . . be there" sooner than he wanted. As we began to sing the familiar strains of the beloved old song, Mr. Jones lifted his head from the pillow and moved to a half-sitting position. By the time we reached the chorus, his hearty, robust voice could be heard out in the hallway. I was certain the Lord must have heard him because everyone on the second floor surely did! A man in the bed across from Mr. Jones's registered amazement, although more as an observer than as a participant in our little music session. We sang several gospel songs, and Mr. Jones sang along as though he were back in his old country church on a Sunday morning. Then he reached up a big hand and stroked the growing stubble on his chin. "Oh my, it's been a mighty long time since I shaved."

As he disappeared into the bathroom to perform his task, his puzzled roommate said, "That music must have worked wonders for him. He's hardly moved in days!"

Vickie and I were still smiling as we walked down the hall. In the distance we heard a faint voice calling out. At first we thought a patient was calling for a nurse, but the request came again: "I want some singing in my room!" We followed the direction of the sound, and at far end of the hall we found a fragile woman in her bed. She appeared to be more bone than flesh. She obviously did not want to engage in small talk. "I want you to sing me the song about the roses," she demanded.

Puzzled, I began suggesting titles that included roses, such as "Moonlight and Roses" and "I'm Sending You a Big Bouquet of Roses."

"No, none of those!" she snapped. "I know you know the song. It goes like this." Suddenly, in a voice much larger than her small frame would seem to indicate, she began to sing, "When the rose's called up yonder, I'll be there." I quickly joined her with the guitar.

I suppressed a giggle as we left the room. "Vickie, I didn't realize how much fun the patients have singing their favorite songs. They don't even need us!"

Sometimes volunteers can get into a bit of trouble when

the patients sing along too. One of our patients, Viro DiJoy, a handsome Italian with flashing dark eyes and curly black hair, had a smile that covered his round, ruddy face. His name means *joy* in his native tongue, and he seemed to radiate that feeling to the entire staff on the second floor. Consequently we all called him "Mr. Joy." He had been critically injured in a truck collision, yet his personality and optimism seemed totally unaffected. The first afternoon I met him, he was lying in bed, smothered in a mountain of casts, with various members of his body suspended in a network of pulleys.

"So, your name is 'Joy'?" I questioned.

"Sure," he replied in a heavy accent. "I come from sunshine country. I'm happy ninety-nine percent of the time."

"That's good, because it's rubbing off on us," I responded, marveling at such a positive attitude despite his recent brush with death. "Maybe you'd better trade in your truck for a bicycle, though."

Laughing heartily, Mr. Joy declared, "I always said horses and buggies were better!"

"I know that all Italians sing, Mr. Joy. Would you mind singing an Italian song for me?"

"I'd love to!" he exclaimed. "I always sing when I'm driving along in my truck. Can I sing 'O Solo Mio'?"

"Why not?" I asked. I was pleased.

I was totally unprepared for a rendition worthy of Caruso, however. Mr. Joy sang with such gusto that I eased toward the door and closed it discreetly. That didn't help. The song started out well enough, but somewhere between the verse and the chorus, Mr. Joy misplaced his pitch. The volume rose to an alarming crescendo as he wandered painfully from note to note, trying desperately to rediscover the right key. The agony of his attempts convinced me that the administrator would momentarily burst through the door to quell the massacre.

After what seemed an eternity, Mr. Joy's voice and my guitar found each other again, and he was back on key. But it was too late to prevent expressions of alarm. The hospital switchboard was directly below Mr. Joy's room. Quickly leaving her post, the switchboard operator dashed up to the second-floor nurses' station and exclaimed, pointing to Mr. Joy's room, "Someone is in terrible pain in that room! Why don't you help him?"

A laughing nurse calmed the startled operator. "Oh, don't worry about Mr. Joy. He's just having a little music therapy."

"My singing was very bad," Mr. Joy said, perplexed, shaking his head. "I never sing so bad before in my life. I make many mistakes. We do the song again, no?"

"Oh, no!" I said emphatically. "I think your song was just fine!"

After weeks of memorable experiences with Mr. Joy, I arrived at the hospital one day to find that he had checked out. A nurse handed me a folded note. "He wanted you to have this," she said.

"Deanna, music is the best medicine for pain," he wrote, "and it has cheered me up. I've had a lot of encounters in my life—you know, bad ones—and music was the best escape from them. While I was sick, you made me feel well. I hope you sing like this forever and ever."

In all of our experiences with music, we never knew of another patient complaining about the noise. Perhaps it is true, as the physician said, that the noise of music is a joyful sound.

Music is a total experience, and we found it helped to alleviate physical as well as emotional pain. By giving patients something positive to involve themselves in, we found their attention would shift from the pain to the music, much as the Lamaze method of childbirth helps a woman in labor to focus away from the pain. We found a surprisingly large number of cases in which patients' direct involvement in music helped them through uncomfortable and difficult moments. Music is not a passive experience. It is an encompassing expression of mind and emotion and serves a unique purpose in patient care. We found that while television programs also helped patients to refocus temporarily, the programs did not provide them with the live presence of a musician or the opportunity to get involved themselves. "The television set can't sing my favorite songs and hold my hand," one patient said. As a result, some of the patients would create their own opportunities.

Mrs. Outlaw, an eighty-seven-year-old patient with a lively mind, had a quick, endearing wit. Laughter had carved lines around her deepset eyes, and snow-white hair wreathed her head in a halo of light. One morning as I entered her room, I remarked brightly, "Mrs. Outlaw, it's good to see you again. How are you doing today?"

"Not too bad, except for the burning." She gestured toward a hollow place in the sheet where her leg had been. "I've got this awful burning—like my leg is still there and it's still on fire."

"You had a leg amputated last week, didn't you?" I asked.

"Yes, a week ago yesterday."

"You've been in and out of the hospital quite a bit, haven't you?"

She nodded. "Three or four times since I first met you."

I looked into her twinkling eyes. "Mrs. Outlaw, may I ask you one question I've been curious about for some time?"

Looking at me expectantly, she said, "Yes?"

"Does anybody ever tease you about your name?"

She chuckled. "I've been called everything but a bank robber, I assure you. 'Holdup,' 'Lawbreaker'—you name it and I've been called it. But you can call me anything you please."

"You know, Mrs. Outlaw, whenever you come into our hospital I look forward to hearing you sing. Would you sing my two favorites today?"

With her voice cracking a bit on the high notes, she sang "There Is Sunshine in My Soul Today" and "The Old Rugged Cross."

"Where did you learn to sing like that?" I asked, sensing that music must have played a major role in her life.

"When I was a kid I loved to sing. I used to work hard, and, you know, the harder I worked the harder I'd sing. I never ran out of a song either, not once!"

"Do you think the music has been helpful to you here at Mennonite Hospital?" I asked.

"I know it has!" Mrs. Outlaw exclaimed. "This burning in my leg—I used to cry a lot when it got too bad. When I'm singing, I don't notice it so much. When you can't come in to sing with me and it's late at night, I sing just the same. I tell the nurses, 'If I want to sing "The Old Rugged Cross," I'm going to sing it. And if you nurses don't like it, you can shut your doors!' "

Memorable musical moments filled the pages of my journal as Vickie and I continued our program one day each week at the hospital. Sometimes we went on weekends to sing for patients who needed us. I was learning to adjust to the new feeling of spending time and conversing with people who were ill. One day, however, something happened that left me feeling useless, helpless, and upset. It led me to the discovery that I was not as prepared to communicate openly and honestly with the patients as I had at first thought.

One afternoon we visited a woman who appeared to be in her middle forties. Her gaunt face reminded me of another face, buried deep in my past. Illness had ravaged her body. There was a haunting loneliness in her eyes. James Taylor's song "You've Got a Friend" seemed right for her, and we sang it with believable warmth. "If you need a friend, just call out my name and I'll be there . . . "

A look of relief spread over her face. Lifting herself in a new burst of energy, she looked as if she were about to leap from her pillows. "How did you know that I'm going to die?"

My knees suddenly felt weak, and I wanted to run from her room. In that moment I saw my father's face and eyes in hers. It was a question my father had never dared to ask me. With Dad, there had been no verbal confrontations with reality. But something in our approach and in the song Vickie and I had sung made our patient believe she could talk about "it" with us—that perhaps we would not be afraid to walk with her for a short time through the final moments of her life. It was, however, a walk I was not prepared to make.

I stumbled through a brief and awkward conversation. Then I said, "We haven't much time today. Maybe we can come back again soon."

As I hastily retreated down the hall, I thought of a patient on the same unit whom I had grown to love. He had a beautiful voice and always sang "How Great Thou Art" with me. His room would be a welcome refuge. When I suggested we sing to him, Vickie stopped abruptly. "I'm sorry," she said, a look of concern spreading across her face. "The patient in that room died last week. I forgot to tell you."

I carried my guitar down to the Activity Therapy Department and tucked it away in its sturdy black case. I said good-bye to the residents and then signed out, unsure that I would be coming back. As I walked through the exit, I began to realize why I had refused Shirley Hoffman so many times. It had been so much easier to say "I don't have time to become a volunteer" than to say "I'm afraid." For the first time in the nine years since my father's death, fear had a name.

4

Singing About Dying

Sensing that something was wrong, Vickie called me a few nights later. "I haven't heard from you for a while, and I'm wondering how you're getting along."

"Vickie, I love our work at the hospital," I said, the words tumbling over each other. "Some of the most meaningful experiences of my life have happened since I began volunteering at Mennonite Hospital. But I'm having a little trouble relating to the patients who are most seriously ill. It's exciting to sing to patients we know will get well and go home. But I guess it never occurred to me that some of the patients will not get well, that some of them will die. I just don't know if I can handle that."

Vickie was perceptive and sympathetic. "Deanna, we need to talk about this. Could you meet me in that little restaurant on Main Street near the hospital tonight at seven?"

That evening Vickie shared some of her own struggles as a student nurse—her ambivalence about really becoming a nurse and her struggle with communication skills, especially with her dying patients. "If you are a sensitive person, it's never going to be easy. Even with all my experience, I still sometimes find myself struggling with what to say and what to do."

"But Vickie," I interrupted, "I don't know if I want to grow close and learn to love people who are going to die. I don't know how to help them or what to say."

"I understand," she said. "There's a risk involved in

reaching out to patients. They need to be more than a room number. They need to know that they have a place in the hearts of those who care for them. In the process of letting them know you love them, you're going to get hurt when the time comes to let go. But, Deanna, there's pain inherent in any meaningful relationship." She smiled as she remembered a humorous incident. "Once a couple came up to me and the wife said glowingly, 'Vickie, my husband and I have been married for forty-seven years and we've never had an argument.' I was tempted to say, 'Then one of you has been dead for forty-seven years.' "

I couldn't help but chuckle to myself. She continued, "It's even harder to establish a deep personal relationship with dying patients because you grieve inside when that relationship ends. But look at the rewards. If you take that risk and jump into the pain with them, they'll teach you things about life you never knew before. And when you're afraid you'll say or do the wrong thing, it won't matter so much because they'll know that at least you're trying and at least you care. In fact, there's much to be said about the joy of caring for the dying. Kahlil Gibran said, 'The deeper that sorrow carves into your being, the more joy you can contain.'

"As health-care professionals and volunteers, we must remember that we are always the students, and the dying patients are the teachers. No longer will we allow the dying to be isolated in a darkened room at the far end of the corridor because they remind us of our own mortality. When we face our own fears of death, we joyously free ourselves to establish a climate of acceptance that enables us to learn how to live better and how to love better. When I walk closely with my dying patients, the joy is mine because I discover life and living as they teach me of death and dying. Because of them, I have become more aware of the little things most of us take for granted. Our patients don't really care how much we know until they know how much we care. Just remember, caring is the only daring."

"Last Thursday I felt so uncomfortable that I wanted to run away," I confessed.

"Deanna, you have so much to give. It would be unfortunate if you allowed fear to stand in your way. I have some books I want you to read. We have so much more information available to us now than we did ten years ago."

Our discussion led me into an in-depth study of a subject many people in our society would find extremely uncomfortable. The writings of such noted authors as Elisabeth Kübler-Ross, with her pioneering efforts, and Robert Fulton, Edgar Jackson, Earl Grollman, and Roy Nichols provided me with much needed insight into the subjects of grief and bereavement. I learned that two of the biggest fears the dying patient has are the fear of being alone and the fear of being forgotten. I learned that communication with a dying patient does not require long, fancy speeches or lengthy conversations about death. It requires openness, honesty, and an ability to look reality in the face and come to grips with it.

When Vickie learned of a five-day retreat on death and dying to be held at Yokefellow Institute in Richmond, Indiana, she suggested we attend the workshop together. Ministers, teachers, nurses, and others involved in the helping professions came from many different states. Several had been assigned to give special presentations. Vickie and I were asked to give short presentations about our music ministry in the hospital.

After lunch we all gathered in a circle in a large, comfortable room and introduced ourselves. Most of us said we were there to help clients, students, patients, and family members. We were not yet fully aware that most of us were also there to help ourselves face our fears and other feelings about our own mortality.

For the most part, the five-day workshop gave us the opportunity to share personal feelings and experiences. Group sessions were held in a round, oak-paneled room. We often gathered around a huge fireplace for song and fellowship.

Midway through the week we had an unforgettable teaching experience, one that seemed to have been prepared especially for me. Dick Baer, a gentle-eyed minister, brought in a book he wanted to discuss titled *Prison to Praise,* by Merlin Carothers. We sat on the floor around him while he shared the book's message and spoke about difficult experiences he had been going through because of a recent divorce. "The great pain of having been rejected by someone you love very deeply, someone with whom you have shared a good deal of life, can be overwhelming," he said. "When I was groping with the most difficult experience of my life, this book appeared in my mailbox. To this day I don't know where it came from. Something compelled me to read it thoroughly. In spite of the rather poor literary style, there was something there that seemed very real. The thesis of the book, summarized quickly, is that one can learn to thank God and praise Him for the darkness in life, for the pain, the hurt, the loneliness, and the difficulties, as well as for the good things. This was very hard for me to understand, and seemed a rather foolish idea when I first encountered it.

"The author goes on to explain that this in no way means that one has to believe that God sends the darkness, or the pain, or the hurt, but that He *permits* them. In no way need we pretend to like what has happened to us in situations of suffering, loss, and pain. But we can learn to thank and to praise God, not just in spite of or in the midst of the hurt, but even *for* the pain and the hurt, the darkness and the loneliness.

"Well," he continued, "I struggled with this concept for a long time, and went back and reread some of it. I didn't understand all the dynamics of the book intellectually, but I am beginning to find out something of what it means. It became real to me when, for the first time, I was able to say, 'Thank you, Lord, for the pain and the hurt. I don't like it. It's a terrible experience to me; but I believe that somehow out of this there is the possibility of even more life, more depth, and more richness in my life.' And I was free! I experienced an amazing change in attitude."

Dick paused, and we sat quietly, thinking about what he had said. Then he went on.

"I have learned that there is indeed some strange relationship that is very hard to figure out between praising God, even for the darkness, and accepting oneself and one's life as it is. I have also found that this can never be a bargain. It can never be 'I will thank God for the pain so the pain will leave me,' or 'I will thank Him for the bad traits in my loved ones so they will change.' This is only a more subtle form of manipulation, and God cannot be manipulated. But in the act of giving praise and thanks for the pain, the hurt, and the suffering—with no bargains—frequently there comes an amazing acceptance of life, of oneself, and of people close to oneself.

"One of the things I have discovered as I've done research over the years is that this theme goes a long way back, even to the biblical writings. Paul, for instance, thanked God for his weakness. This is a strange phenomenon. He said, 'I glory in my weakness because this gives God the opportunity to work through me. It gives life the possibility of flowing through me!' These experiences led me to begin to explore the subject of praising God for all things in a more systematic and scholarly fashion. Romans 8:28 says that God works everything for good with those who love him, according to His purpose. Helen Keller once said, 'I thank God for my handicaps, for through them I have found myself, my work and my God.'

"Gradually, I expanded my studies to include poetry, philosophy, and literature, and discovered some beautiful passages in the writings of Ranier Maria Rilke, Arthur Miller, and others. I'm amazed, as I see in these writings, at the possibility of letting go so that we no longer insist on having the focused, objective, analytical part of the mind totally rule the person. And one of the things I think is happening is that thanking God even for the darkness is, in a sense, a terrible offense to the analytical mind. The need to be in control, to understand everything, to say, 'I won't accept unless I understand,' or 'I won't praise God for the suffering unless I know exactly what is going to come out of this,' is very real.

"But one of the things that happens in this seemingly foolish act of thanking God for the darkness, the pain, and the loneliness is that the domination, the lopsided commitment to the analytical, objectifying mind and its functions, is broken. It is really a letting go. The discovery that we really can let go, and that there is something there that catches us, can be freeing. There is a power in life itself that is there, and that is saying in big capital letters 'YES!' to our lives in that moment of letting go.

"The kind of praise I'm talking about, then, is no Pollyanna optimism. It's no stock denial of the suffering of the world. It doesn't need to pretend that Dachau and Auschwitz or the napalming of Vietnamese children never happened. In fact, most of the people I know who have broken through to genuine and lasting praise for adversity in their lives are people who have suffered deeply, people who have known evil, have encountered it directly and brutally, and yet somehow have gone beyond the impact of that evil to quiet acceptance.

"The reason that Christians and Jews can speak so freely about praise without becoming callous and indifferent to the suffering of the world is that they know—through their own traditions, through the image of the suffering servant in Judaism, and through the reality of the crucifixion in Christianity—what suffering means. Thus, we don't have to become indifferent to the cries of little children and to the pangs of nature brutalized because of man's greed and indifference. We don't have to ignore the cries of third-world mothers who watch their children's bodies and minds twisted by hunger and malnutrition, for biblical religion is rooted in suffering. Christianity is rooted in the cross as well as in the Resurrection.

"I've come to believe that God is precisely the one who always remembers the good and transforms the evil in our lives. Whenever there is beauty, truth, nobility, strength, courage, hope, love, kindness, and freedom, God remembers these and somehow writes them into the very fabric of the universe. But He does this through Christ, who always takes the suffering, the pain, the loneliness, and the hurt of human existence back into Himself, and who, through what one writer has called the 'alchemy of grace,' transforms these (if we will let Him) into the possibility of new life, into the seedbed of the future. The suffering and the pain and the disappointment become the fertilizer for the future. If we will give Him back our pain and our suffering—indeed, if we can even learn to praise Him for permitting pain to happen in our lives—I believe we will see miracles happen!"

When Dick finished, there was silence in the room for a few minutes, and I felt the awareness of a profound truth growing in my mind. Scriptural passages became clearer to me—teachings about how important it is that there be opposition in all things. Pain . . . Death . . . The possibility of new growth and new life . . .

Is it true, I wondered, *that we should not always strive to be "on top of the world"?* The view from the mountaintop is beautiful, but so is the view from the valley as we gaze up at the giant peaks. If we could allow ourselves to pass more comfortably through the valleys and shadows of our lives, and even to thank God for those valleys and shadows, wouldn't that lead to greater personal growth? But could I do it? Could I learn to thank God for all the past hurts and for the rejection that taught me acceptance and the pain that taught me compassion? I thought of something I had read long ago, about the importance of viewing pain as a teacher and not just an enemy:

> Pain stayed so long I said to him today—"Be gone! I will not have you with me anymore!" I stamped my foot and paused there, startled at the look he wore. "I who have been your friend?" he said to me. "I who have been

> your teacher? All that you know of understanding, love, sympathy, and patience, I have taught you. Shall I go?" He spoke the truth, this strange, unwelcome guest. I watched him leave and knew that he was wise. He left a heart grown tender in my breast and a far clearer vision in my eyes. I dried my tears and lifted up a song—even for one who had tortured me so long. (Author unknown.)

Darkness fits into the total symphony of my life, I thought, trying to capture and hold the analogy in musical terms that were most meaningful to me. Life itself, with its mountains and valleys, its light and its darkness, is like a symphony with its crescendos and diminuendos, its dissonance and resolutions. Today, because of Dick, I had been able to hear more of the symphony.

As we were leaving the Oak Room, Dick handed me the book *Prison to Praise.* "Here, I want you to have this," he said. "I hope it will mean as much to you as it has to me."

The following evening Dick Obershaw, a grief counselor from Minnesota, approached me. A sensitive man with a casual, down-to-earth approach, Dick looked directly at me, his eyes penetrating, and said, "Deanna, you only briefly mentioned your father's death this week, and I'm interested in learning more about that experience."

"I went to visit my father when he was ill," I responded, "but beyond that I can't tell you a great deal about his death. After he was admitted to the hospital, I didn't see him again."

Dick raised an eyebrow and probed a bit further. "You didn't see your father at all after he died? Didn't you attend his funeral?"

"No. I didn't go to his funeral," I admitted, feeling somewhat uncomfortable with the admission that I had not attended such a significant event.

"Why didn't you go?"

"I wasn't feeling well."

"Were you ill? Why didn't you feel well?" he pressed.

My discomfort had turned to a feeling of annoyance. He was asking about a very personal matter, and I certainly did not owe him any explanations. "I don't really remember all the reasons," I said. I quickly changed the subject. "Are you going swimming with the group tonight?"

Sensing he had gone far enough, Dick answered, "Sure, I'll see you there."

That evening, while everyone was noisily splashing about, I sat by the edge of the pool, staring into the water. I kept seeing Dad's face reflected on the shiny surface. Why didn't I go to his funeral? Why didn't I have the courage to say good-bye?

It was my first real awareness that I had a problem. I had always thought that faith transcended the need to grieve. Grief had been spoken of at the conference as "hard work" or "love work." Had I been using my faith in life after death as a reason to avoid doing my grief work? Was it work I had been unable or simply unwilling to do? If there was unfinished business, unfinished grief work for my father's death, could I still do that work after nine years? If I could, would that make it easier to communicate with dying patients at Mennonite Hospital? For the first time in many days I was not afraid to say "I'm afraid."

Later that evening some of us gathered around the fireplace in the Oak Room. I quietly strummed the guitar. Sandy, a young mother who had just lost her husband, sat staring into the flames, Vickie was sitting nearby, and Dick Obershaw was stretched out on the floor, his head resting against the cushion of a chair.

"Sometimes it can be easier to sing than to talk," Dick said, without looking directly at me. "Sometimes guitars can build walls instead of bridges."

Touched by his wisdom, I knew that my own moment to share had come. Without hesitation I put down my guitar and began to retrace my steps on the long road leading into yesterday. I described how Dad looked when he turned toward me in the room where he was being cared for, and how I felt when I began to realize he was dying. I shared the story of the tumultuous years before his illness, my ambivalent feelings about him as I was growing up, and my yearning to have a father in the home. I talked about the imaginary heroes I had created to replace him, and how I had come to finally know, to love, and to accept the person he was.

As I talked about the hardest part, the verbal isolation during his illness and my refusal to attend his funeral, I felt warm tears falling down my cheeks. I was crying for the lost moments and the unfulfilled dreams. I was crying for my Dad for the first time since his death, and it was okay. The tears felt good.

"When we recognize unresolved grief, wonderful lessons can be learned," Dick said gently. "There may be another father figure who comes into your life someday, someone who is dying. If that happens, be there for him. Do all the things you didn't do for your own father. That will help to heal the hurt. It may be a friend, a patient, a family member. And when that happens, give yourself the freedom to feel and to respond to the loss. Say yes to the pain. Try to be there for all the hurting people who need you. And as you help them, you'll find that the experience with your father was not lost at all. It will have become a great learning experience for you, a great teaching tool. You can't go back into the past and change your response to what happened, but you *can* change your response to what happens now."

He paused for a moment, then asked, "Deanna, if you could go back to that long summer, sit at your father's bedside, and have a conversation with him once more, what would you say?"

All at once I found myself sitting again at Dad's bedside, with no guitar between us to fill the silence. What I wanted to say was simple. I wanted, most of all, to say, "Thank you." I began to speak, more to Dad than to the group.

"Thank you, Dad, for all the gifts you gave me that you couldn't buy. I know you didn't send child support, and Mother hated you for that. Maybe she always will. But you gave me some gifts that will always be a part of my life. You helped me to love people and to believe in their inherent goodness. You were always optimistic, and when everyone complained about the snowstorms, you'd say, 'Look how gently the arms of the trees are holding the snow.'

"People still say I wear rose-colored glasses, and I suppose I do, but they've helped me to see the harsh world in a soft and shining light. You taught me to have a dream and to hold onto it, even if it didn't come true. You helped me develop my love for nature, for waterfalls, and for wild flowers. But I wish you hadn't taught me to love fried chicken and donuts. That's been a problem.

"Most of all, I want to thank you for cultivating my love for music. I'll remember all those songs you taught me that I can teach now to my children. Dad, music has been such a great blessing in my life. It has helped me to feel that I have a special gift to give to the world. I know we have to say good-bye now, but I know we'll meet again. And, Dad, I'll miss you so much . . ."

We sat in silence and watched the flames dance over the crackling logs, and I began to think how important what I had just said would have been to my father. To a wounded, broken man who felt he had failed his family, what would those words have meant to him?

Dick, his eyes misty with tears, finally said, "Somehow, Deanna, I believe, after all, that your father heard you."

Putting myself in my father's place, going back to his bedside in memory, was an unforgettable experience. If he felt alone and isolated, I concluded, there were probably thousands of others who felt the same way. I thought that if I could capture all the feelings in music, if I could put my father's needs into a song, perhaps it would help other people to communicate more openly and honestly with their dying loved ones and help them avoid making the mistakes I had made. And so it was that a song was born in Richmond, a song that all the participants sang together when we said good-bye, titled "Teach Me to Die":

Sunlight filters through my window, falling from the sky.
Time slips like a silent stranger, softly passing by.

Life goes on in busy circles, leaving me behind.
Memories, like portraits, fill the attic of my mind.

I know that it isn't easy seeing me this way
And it hurts to watch me lying here day after day.
Trade your fear of parting for the faith that knows no pain.
Don't be afraid to say good-bye—I know we'll meet again!

Teach me to die. Hold onto my hand.
I have so many questions—things I don't understand.
Teach me to die. Give all you can give.
If you'll teach me of dying, I will teach you to live!

The song was carried by my fellow workshop participants to their various states and fast became a musical resource for workshops on death and dying. It was used in slide presentations by volunteers involved in the national hospice movement, volunteers who assist family members in caring for terminally ill loved ones at home. Calls began to come in from organizations wanting me to give workshops, using music as a teaching tool. I discovered that the song not only gave dying patients a musical voice, it also was a gentle, nonthreatening way to teach about a difficult subject. After the workshop in Richmond, I found it was easier for me to relate both to patients and to audiences.

The growing interest in a song that gently confronted the experience of dying led to my decision to try to find a publisher for it. I began sending copies to publishing companies in Chicago, New York, and Los Angeles, and everywhere I met with the same response: "Most producers in the music business don't even want to think about death, much less sing about it. We're sorry. It's just not commercial."

I quickly learned that only three basic subjects are addressed in commercial music literature: falling in love, slippin' around, and falling out of love. People who are sick, elderly, or dying have been left in a musical void. Becoming increasingly discouraged with the prospect of finding a publisher, I was ready to shelve the project when I learned that NBC News was going to do a television special on a book written by Elisabeth Kübler-Ross titled *On Death and Dying*. The program was to be sponsored by the United Catholic Conference, and I received an invitation to submit the song for use in the program as credits were running at the end.

At the taping, which took place in Chicago, I met Joan Paul, production manager for the United Catholic Conference. A striking, slender woman, Joan was a wonderful combination of warmth and dignity. Our rapport was instantaneous. After the song had been recorded, Joan approached me, her voice rich with excitement. "There's a great need in the world for a song like 'Teach Me To Die,' " she said. "It reflects the feelings of so many dying patients. I'm wondering if you have a publisher for it."

I stood speechless. There was no way Joan could have known of my futile search for someone who believed in the message and recognized the need to publish it.

"If you ever need an agent for the song, please let me know," Joan added. She promised to do everything in her power to find a publisher for it.

In late December, I received a letter from Joan that sent my spirits soaring. "Deanna," she wrote, "I recently played your song for several groups of people at a communications conference in Detroit, and I am certain that the Franciscan Communications Center in Los Angeles would be interested. Even among the people in Detroit last weekend, there were offers to use the song on local radio and television shows, at death and dying seminars, and in classrooms. Please trust me that this is the best route to go. I am convinced that for the song to succeed, it must be handled by spiritually motivated people who believe in it and who want to use it for good."

Shortly afterward, I received my first letter from Cullen Schippe, director of recording for the Franciscan Communications Center and also a producer of resources for the elderly. Cullen told me that the center was very excited about the music and that he would be in touch again as soon as their creative committee had listened to it.

After the hearing I spoke with Cullen on the phone. The committee had approved the project, he said. Then he suggested that we record an album instead of a single. The sudden awareness that I could write songs for patients without worrying about the music's commercial appeal filled me with a sense of relief. We could at last give them a musical voice.

My husband offered his wholehearted support from the beginning. After signing a recording contract with the Franciscan Communications Center, I went to work writing additional songs, and Cullen began the task of finding adequate funding. The Franciscans are among the country's largest producers of religious audiovisual materials, but they are a nonprofit organization and depend on donations from outside groups to fund their projects. Knowing of our urgent need, Father Tony Scannell, president of the Franciscan Communications Center, sent out a letter to patrons, telling them about my work and about our hopes and dreams to see the album completed.

Soon thereafter, Father Scannell received a letter from an elderly woman who was poor and in need of help herself. She wrote about how she had taken music to her own mother who lay dying in a hospital, and how much she believed in music as therapy. She sent a donation of one dollar. "The widow's mite!" exclaimed Father Tony as he shared her letter with me. Her letter touched us all and made us even more determined to get funding for our project.

One of our greatest fans was to be Cullen's father, who was dying of cancer in a hospital in Milwaukee, Wisconsin. Cullen and his father had been having a great deal of trouble communicating during his illness. I empathized when Cullen confided, "Deanna, sometimes I think I withdraw from Dad because I don't want to face it. It isn't that I'm insensitive to his needs or that I don't love him deeply. I just don't know quite how to handle my own feelings about the fact that he may not have much time left to live. Maybe getting involved in the message of your music will help me do this."

One day when Cullen was talking with his father on the

phone, he said, "Dad, we still don't have enough funding for the album and I don't know what we're going to do. I haven't got twenty thousand dollars lying around. Dad, could you pray up some for us?" Calmly, from his bed at Deaconess Hospital, his father replied, "Sure, son."

One month to the day after their conversation, Cullen called again. "You'll never guess what I have in my hand. It's a check for twenty-five thousand dollars! The big irony is where this check came from. It's from a foundation that has its offices directly across the street from Deaconess Hospital, where Dad is. My father had never talked about the foundation, didn't even know it was there."

A recording date was set, and Cullen secured the services of a talented young arranger, Ed Lojeski. Together they enlisted the help of some of California's finest musicians. Ed's uncle, Harry Lojewski, supervisor of music at MGM Studios, agreed to supervise our session. During our first meeting he said, "Deanna, if I could give you one bit of advice before we go into the studio, it would be this: Sing as if you were singing to only one person, and when people hear it, they'll feel as if it's being sung to them alone."

I will never forget my first glimpse of the Franciscan Communication Center on Santee Street in Los Angeles. I squinted and looked up at an unpretentious, massive building in the middle of a parking lot. It bore only one decoration that I could see, but it was enough to make me feel right at home. Just above the front door, in colorful inlay, was the symbol of a dove. A Peacebird.

Elisabeth Kübler-Ross had shared, during the NBC News special, the story of a little boy who was dying of a malignant brain tumor. I thought of that and knew what the theme song of the album would be. Shortly before his death, the little boy had drawn a picture of a bird soaring skyward with yellow crayon on its wings. It was symbolic of his feelings about his approaching death. "This is the Peacebird," he said, "and I'm flying through the sky with the sunlight on my wings."

His courage and child's wisdom inspired me to write the song "Peacebird."

Cullen took me on a tour of the building and told me about the work that was done there and the purposes behind it. "This is where we do much of our filming and storing of props," he said as we entered what looked like a mammoth gymnasium. "There is so much that can be done in the film and music industries to make people aware of the needs of others. I see a lot of pain and suffering in the world, not just the pain of death and loss, but the pain people have from not being loved, from being hungry, from being a different color and therefore the recipients of bias and hatred. Sometimes I'm overwhelmed by a sense of helplessness, and I feel a strong need to address those problems. Remember when we record, Deanna, that if we can make life or death easier for just one person, it will have been worth all our efforts."

We walked past the film settings and props. "Isn't it a challenge to come up with so many new ideas for films and television spots?" I asked.

"Yes, it is a challenge," Cullen said. "We have a very creative staff here. We shoot thousands of feet of film during hours of work, and yet we use very little of it after the final editing. Our goal is to condense and package the message, to say the most with the fewest words. We just want people to hear the sounds of love and see love in action. We want them to know that in the midst of their pain and problems, love works. That's basically all we do here."

If that was all they did there, it was a great service. The Franciscans love their work and each other. They are extraordinary ordinary people working every day to make the world a little more thoughtful, a little more loving. Their award-winning films about human needs are appropriate for use by any religious denomination.

Our recording sessions took approximately a week, with musicians laying down their soundtracks first. Then I worked on vocals, using earphones so I could hear the orchestration. Because of the high cost of studio time, it was important that we work efficiently. It was fun getting to know the musicians, many of whom came casually dressed in old clothes and funny hats. The tiny peacebird pins I had distributed appeared on collars, hats, and pockets.

We learned that many of the people involved in our recording sessions were having their own problems coping with loss and illness, so our sessions were also therapy. One of the musicians had leukemia; another had just lost his wife. The recording engineer had a friend who was gravely ill, as was Cullen's father. Cullen told me that involvement in the project had opened lines of communication between him and his father that otherwise might never have occurred.

Several days of intensive work culminated in the most moving moment for me when we finally recorded the song "Teach Me to Die." I stood in the recording booth wearing headphones, the soft strains of flutes and wind chimes filling my ears. I thought of the note Joan Paul had given me to read just before recording the songs: "Deanna, you are now realizing one of your fondest dreams. We will all be thinking of you, joining you in spirit, knowing that you are doing something beautiful for God." I could hardly contain the emotion that swept through me. "This one's for you, Dad," I whispered. "This one's for you."

Soon after we finished the song, a reporter arrived at the studio to do a story for the Los Angeles *Times*. As soon as she left, a call was put through to the control room. It was for Cullen. His mother was calling from Deaconess Hospital in Milwaukee. His father had taken a turn for the worse, and Cullen would have to come as soon as possible.

Cullen's father died in his arms the day the Los Angeles *Times* printed the story about our album. Cullen later confided, "My father's death was, for me, a beautiful experience. I treasure every moment of it. I say that advisedly, because for my Dad, who understood that he was dying, it meant an end to suffering. We could look into each other's eyes and know that we loved each other, that we cared about each other. Oh, we cried a lot, but we rejoiced in it. We grew with it. And we can live today because of that moment."

When the album was finished, "Peacebird" became the title song. Its sensitive message conveyed well what we were trying to say, that peace often comes through adversity and that there is indeed a spirit, a light within:

Hanging by a silver thread
Between the earth and sky,
A fragile end he couldn't understand.
I hurled my angry questions
Through the emptiness of time
And then I saw the picture in his hand.

No earthbound fears could stay the tears
That glistened in my eyes
And fell upon the picture that he drew;
But stealing through my consciousness,
The golden light of peace
Fell softly on the memories we knew.

Drawn by a hand so small,
High over mountains tall,

Music Brings My Heart Back Home

I hear the echo as it sings.
Lost in the distant skies,
Found in a child's eyes,
The Bird of Peace
With sunlight on its wings!

5

Just a Memory Away

"United Flight 103 is now ready for boarding!"

I was at O'Hare International Airport in Chicago, on my way to Catonsville, Maryland, to attend a workshop on coping with loss. A nurse I had met at the Richmond workshop would be meeting my plane at Washington National Airport.

As I walked past the Chicago newspaper stands lined side by side in the corridor, a headline caught my attention. It read "Facing Death He Finds Fame." I stopped abruptly, turned, and went back to read the headline again. "Orville Kelly: Facing Death He Finds Fame." I was irritated by the headline, which seemed to assume that fame was supposed to be some sort of compensation for a man's impending death. But I decided to buy the newspaper. It was all I needed—one more thing to carry—but there was something haunting in the eyes of the man in the photograph and the family gathered about him.

When we were airborne, I pulled out the paper and began to read the story. I became even more irritated by the newspaper reporter's first line: "Burlington, Iowa—Since he learned he has terminal cancer, 43-year-old Orville Kelly has been having the time of his life."

I grimaced, wondering if the insensitive reporter would have enjoyed trading places with the man in the story. A newspaperman, Mr. Kelly faced major problems after being told he had incurable cancer spreading through his lymph system. Initially, he lost interest in everything and experienced a growing preoccupation with death and depression. He spent most of his time in his study, lying down, facing a dark and uncertain future. "I couldn't even yell at the kids when they got out of line," the article quoted Kelly as saying. "All I could do was sit and stare and wonder why God was doing this to me."

His depression began to affect his family, even though his four children had not been told of the cancer. When he was placed on chemotherapy, it meant long drives to Iowa City Hospital for treatments. One autumn day, as Kelly and his wife, Wanda, were driving back to Burlington after one of his treatments, he noticed a look of terrible despair on her face. It finally occurred to him that he was drawing his family into his own depression, that they were almost dying with him. At that moment he decided to stop thinking about dying and start thinking about living.

Kelly told his wife that they were going to go home and have an old-fashioned barbecue, just like old times, and that he was going to tell the children about his cancer. That evening he drew thirteen-year-old Mark, eleven-year-old Tammy, eight-year-old Lori, and four-year-old Britt to him. "I have cancer," he told them. "Cancer. And I'll probably die of it. But I'm not dead yet! We have a lot of living to do. Sometimes things may get bad, but I want you all to help me live with this. We don't have to like death, but we don't have to be terrified by it either."

A few days later Kelly wrote an article for the Burlington newspaper telling how it felt to have a terminal illness. After the story appeared, letters came in from many other patients and their families. Because of their reaction, he decided to start an organization for persons with life-threatening illnesses and their families.

The first meeting was held January 25, 1974, in the Burlington Elks Lodge. The eighteen people who attended decided to call the group "Make Today Count." At their third meeting, almost fifty persons attended, including clergymen, nurses, and others interested in terminal illness.

"We cry, but we also laugh a lot," Kelly explained. "We talk about each other's illnesses, but we also talk about going fishing. The idea is just to be normal."

Kelly's newspaper story was picked up by the Associated Press, and soon thousands of letters were pouring in from all over the country. People began forming chapters of Make Today Count in their own states. Dictating letters, giving lectures, and answering the phone became a large part of Kelly's life. His family and friends became much more comfortable around him, and they seemed to celebrate every day as if it were a priceless gift. When one of his daughter's classmates said to her at school, "I read in the paper that your Daddy is dying of cancer," she responded, "But he's not dead yet!"

Aside from the innuendos, the newspaper article was an intensely moving story. A group like Make Today Count would have been a great help to me when my own father was dying. I decided that someday I would meet Orville Kelly and share some of my songs with him. That resolution led to a phone call several months later. By the time I was able to reach Mr. Kelly, it was late and his voice sounded tired. "We just returned from the Virgin Islands," he said, "and what I need is a good, long rest."

"Mr. Kelly, I read about your organization, Make Today Count, in a Chicago newspaper and was very moved by the article. I wish your organization had been around when my own father was dying. I recently recorded a song I wrote for my father and wondered if I could share it with you. Do you have a moment?"

I sang the song, "Teach Me to Die," to Orville Kelly. Afterward there was a brief moment of silence, and then Mr. Kelly was back on the line. "That was beautiful," he said softly. "I don't believe I have ever heard a song like it. I want my wife, Wanda, to hear it. Would you mind singing it again, this time for both of us?"

After listening a second time, he said, "I once received a letter from a young girl in Wisconsin. She said people were

willing to talk with her about many things, but not about death. She was a cancer patient. 'I love my parents and they have taught me many things,' she wrote, 'but no one will teach me to die.' " Then he added, "I'm having a birthday party August 2, and some of my closest friends are coming for a little celebration in our home. Could you join us?"

"I'd love to," I said.

"Bring your guitar," he added. "And plan to stay overnight with us. I've written a booklet of poems. If you'll give me your address, I'd like to send you a copy."

On August 2, Orville Kelly's forty-fourth birthday, I drove along the highway through Peoria, past Galesburg, and on toward the Mississippi. A few days earlier, I had read Mr. Kelly's booklet of poems. Now it was easier to understand the thoughts he expressed: "Somehow the depression fades away like the darkness before the coming dawn when I look across the rooftops of Burlington, out across the Mississippi River, and watch the sun burst across the horizon."

Orville Kelly lived in an old house that had a distinct feeling of "home." I rang the doorbell, and almost immediately he answered. His was a commanding presence. It was not just the size of this large, outgoing man that struck me. He was also casual and unpretentious, and there was something unique, perhaps heroic, in his nature. He had straight black hair, a deep cleft in his chin, and brooding dark eyes. He was a man to be remembered.

He greeted me warmly and escorted me past the front room and into a dining area, where more than a dozen people surrounded a large table laden with food. In the center was a birthday cake decorated with the words "Happy Birthday Kelly."

"I never did like the name Orville," he explained. "Just call me Kelly." At that moment Wanda came in carrying a basket of fruit. She smiled when she saw me. "Here's Deanna!" she exclaimed. "I'm so glad you could be with us tonight. We've been looking forward to meeting you." She was youthful and petite, a marked contrast to her large-framed husband. They were very attentive to each other.

The aroma of barbequed meat drifted in from the back porch, and we followed it to fill our plates. Kelly seemed more involved with the people than with the food.

After dinner, we wandered out to the back porch for fresh air and singing. The coals were dying on the grills, and a single star stood out against the sky. I thought of Kelly's poem "River Song" and asked if he would recite it. His voice was pensive as his words slipped out into the darkness . . .

Look at the Mississippi River from the banks of
Burlington
At midnight, if you want to see it.
Add a wisp of fog and a sliver of silver moon
Looking down on a string of barges,
The lights of a farmhouse off in the distance.
This is the way you look at the Mississippi River.

"You have a gift for writing, and for reciting, too," I commented. "Where did you get such a feeling for poetry?"

"I used to live in an old farmhouse in rural Iowa," Kelly explained. "My grandparents raised me. Grandfather was a sharecropper, and I remember when we could fit every possession we had on the old farm wagon. It was during the depression, but I didn't know we were poor. I didn't see that many houses, and the nearest farm was miles away. But oh, the solitude in those woods! Even back then I wanted to write, but I didn't know it.

"I went to a country school that had only about ten kids, and I remember one Christmas my teacher, Miss Briggs, autographed a book for me. She wrote: 'To Orville, Merry Christmas. Miss Briggs, 1939.' I'll never forget her. A teacher can touch your life forever. Miss Briggs inspired me to read, and I read everything I could get my hands on, including all the books in Grandma's attic, from old *Liberty* magazines to the Sears Roebuck catalogs. I had read every story, every advertisement, over and over again, because it was all new to me.

"There was poetry in me then, but I didn't know how to express it. I would feel it and smell it and touch it, not just see it," he continued. "That was the worst of all—seeing it, feeling it, and touching it and not being able to tell anyone about it. Then I began to find in poetry that other poets shared my thoughts. In their lines I could read some of my own feelings, like the poem by Robert Frost, 'Stopping by Woods on a Snowy Evening.' I could just see it. I could visualize those woods. The first real book I ever read that brought it all home to me was Thomas Wolfe's *Time and the River*. It was the first book that gave me the real inspiration to become a writer. When I read that, I just knew I had to tell somebody how I felt."

Memories and melodies blended in with the crisp night air, and all of us were much more aware because of the presence of this man who had so much to give. He asked me to sing some of the songs I had written and then asked if I knew the song "Bobby McGee."

"Certainly," I said. "Why do you like that song?" It was a question I often asked patients. It was important for me to know the memories and feelings behind their requests.

"Before I came to Burlington, I was living in Sterling, Illinois," he said, settling down into the sagging couch. Wanda curled up under his arm. "I knew something was physically wrong with me, but I didn't know it was cancer, so that one-year period in Sterling represents the last real time in my life when I considered myself still healthy, and certainly not 'terminal.' We lived in an older home with a wonderful outside patio and a swimming pool for the children.

"One night in December, when the snow was falling, I decided to stop for a while at a lounge. A young man was singing some of Kris Kristopherson's songs. There was something unique about the night and the music. The young man's girlfriend, Bobbie, was there with him. I invited this couple to stop at our home after he was through playing. They came by, and we sat in front of a glowing fireplace in my living room and listened to the words of 'Me and Bobby McGee.' Whenever I hear the words and the music, I think of that particular night, and the snow, and the feeling that everything was still all right. The scene will never be recreated except in my mind, which is as it should be, I suppose. Perhaps it could easily have been another song, but it wasn't."

After singing "Bobby McGee," I sang Kelly's other favorites: "Mr. Tambourine Man" (the Tambourine Man could represent death, Kelly explained) and "Bridge over Troubled Waters."

"That song is very special to those who are going through

difficult experiences," he said. "I want you to sing that song at my funeral."

Kelly recited some of his poetry that night, as well as some of the great classics. "A poem that's very meaningful to me," he said, "is 'I Have a Rendezvous with Death' by Alan Seeger." He then shared the words with us. He spoke with the voice of a man who had far more to say than time would ever permit. I could almost see the face of the "silent companion" as the message collided with the moment.

> I have a rendezvous with Death
> At some disputed barricade
> When Spring comes round with rustling shade
> And apple blossoms fill the air. . . .
> When Spring trips north again this year,
> And I to my pledged word am true,
> I shall not fail that rendezvous.

The words hung heavy on the still night air. Some of the guests began to move restlessly, and a few prepared to leave.

"I'll get some more refreshments," Wanda said, disappearing into the kitchen.

Kelly chuckled knowingly, then looked into the endless night. "Have you ever wondered what it would be like if your fondest wish could be granted?" he asked.

"If you could have one wish, what would it be?" I responded.

"I'd wish that I could live long enough to see one more snowflake."

I caught my breath. My childhood wishes had been so grandiose—to be able to fly, or to live in a gingerbread house, or to turn into Cinderella for a day. The profound simplicity of Kelly's wish reminded me of how our values and priorities would change if we could only begin to comprehend our own mortality.

Suddenly Kelly's piercing eyes caught mine. "Deanna, when you look at me, what do you see?"

All evening I had the distinct impression that he was testing me to see if I could really listen to him without running away. So far I had passed the tests, but this time he caught me off guard. Why was he asking *me* this question? Why not one of his other guests? He hardly knew me. But I knew that the response I was about to share mattered to him. He had been called the "Cancer Man" in numerous newspaper articles, and cancer meant death. It was absurd. How could I say, "When I look at you I see death"? In my life there had been a growing concept of death as "peace." That sounded better. I stammered a moment, then boldly said, "When I look at you, I see peace."

My words registered more in his mind than in his heart. His face was blank, his eyes expressionless. For this huge man with a message for us all, peace was not the answer. If not peace, then what? Suddenly I knew. "Kelly, when I look at you I see *life,*" I blurted out, wanting to put a capital *L* on *Life.*

His face dissolved into a wide grin. "Thank heavens *somebody* sees life!" he exclaimed. "When people look at me, most of them see a dying man. But I want you to know that I am more alive than anyone in this room. I hear everything. I see everything. *And nothing escapes me.*"

As the evening wore on, I had the uncanny feeling I was beginning to look at life through Kelly's eyes. "I want to live that way too," I said. "You know, with awareness."

"It wasn't always that way for me," he commented. "I didn't even notice I had a lilac bush outside my window until they told me I had cancer. I had to have cancer before I learned what it was to reach out and touch people and to really care for them. Did you know that the mortality rate for every generation is one hundred percent? That lilac bush will have to die someday. Everything dies sometime. But today I'm alive. I still have *now.* Make Today Count doesn't mean you leap out of bed in great spirits every morning and embrace everyone. It doesn't mean you'll never get discouraged. It means that you begin to look upon every day not as another day closer to death, but as another day to live as fully as possible. It doesn't mean that you're *dying* of cancer, but rather that you're learning to *live with it.*"

"I can see why it's so important to look at life that way, even if you aren't sick," I commented.

"When you realize you're not going to live on this earth forever, you begin to notice the little things so much more," Kelly said. "My life is measured by moments now, not years. Now it's measured by a smile on the face of my little boy, a sunrise, a snowflake, an autumn leaf, the touch of a hand. These are the things that make my life worth living."

After the other guests had departed and the table had been cleared, Kelly stretched out on the sofa in his den. The room was dark, and we sat listening to the sounds of train whistles in the distance and barges moving up and down the river.

"What do you want to know about me?" Kelly asked, the evidence of trust in his voice. "I've never granted a total interview. Ask me anything tonight and I'll tell you."

"We wrote our own epitaphs once at a workshop," I said with amusement. "Over the past few months I've heard some interesting ones. One participant said, 'I'm having a great time. Wish you were here.' Another was from a dentist who said, 'I'm filling my last cavity.' Still another from a good friend said, 'I *told* you I was sick.' Then there was the epitaph, 'Somehow in my case I thought an exception would be made'! " Our laughter filled the room, and then I continued. "I think my favorite came from Father Hugh Noonan, who founded the Franciscan Communications Center. He said simply, 'I'm glad I was here.' "

"Beautiful!" exclaimed Kelly. He thought for a moment and then said, "Here's mine: 'He lived. He loved. He died.' What more is there to say?"

"If you could teach me something about communication skills for cancer patients, what would it be?" I asked. "First of all, the negative comments. What are some of the things people say that irritate you?"

"Well, I think it's irritating when people come up with

so much small talk that they avoid talking about things that really mean something," Kelly said. "Seriously speaking, if there is one thing I've learned, it is to cast aside the petty things, the things that don't matter any more. It bothers me when people say, 'I understand exactly how you feel.' They don't know that. I don't know how *they* feel. There's no way I can really know how another person feels.

"People write me fifty-page letters because they are patients, or because they are losing someone they love, and tell me things they would never say to a husband or wife. They identify with the fact that I'm a cancer patient, and they know they'll probably never have to face me, so they pour out their hearts. They write, 'Here's how I feel. I hurt from crying. I'm tired of seeing the blood on the pajamas of my little boy. I don't want them to hurt him anymore.' These are the important things, Deanna."

I nodded. He paused, then continued, "It's irritating to hear people say, 'If you ever need anything, just let me know.' If I said to them, 'Listen, I need *you*,' they wouldn't like it. Are we as willing to give *ourselves* as any *thing?* Can we give up a football game or a hot dinner at home to sit with a dying patient? Another thing I get tired of hearing is, 'Kelly, your cancer is God's will.' One day my minister, who is very sensitive, said to me, 'Kelly, I think that cancer is God's enemy, and I think he's hurting with you.' I can't tell you how much that meant to me. I can understand a God like that.

"If people say, 'Good morning, Kelly. How are you feeling?' and I say, 'I was up all night vomiting, the Cytoxin is bothering me, and I feel lousy,' I can imagine a reply like, 'Oh, great. I'm glad to hear you're feeling better.' " He chuckled. "They're not going to hear that vomiting business. They don't really want to know how I feel. I could lie and say, 'I'm feeling fine.' It would make them more comfortable. If they say, 'Gosh, you're looking good,' why are they saying it? They don't know what else to say! They don't want to say, 'Kelly, you're looking horrible,' even if it's the truth. But you know something? I'd rather have them say that. I really would.

"There were times when I was looking horrible. I was lying in a bed in a hospital once in Iowa City, and the doctors had some trouble with the bone-marrow biopsy, and I was hurting! One of the needles had stuck in my right side, and they had a heck of a time pulling it out. Then from nowhere, two student nurses came in and wanted me to autograph something I had written. But it didn't bother me, really. I needed somebody there. I said, 'I'll give you my autograph if you'll sit down and talk a minute.' What if they had said, 'Kelly, you're looking great today'?"

I had another question. "What if someone says, 'Kelly, you've got twenty years ahead of you'?" I wanted to know because I had heard a guest say that to him before leaving the party.

"I'm turned off by it," Kelly responded. "I don't have twenty years left. How do I know that? How do I know that I'm never going to be president of the United States? How do I know that I'll never fly a jet airplane myself? I can ride in it, but I'm never going to pilot it. The odds are very great that I'm not going to live twenty years. How in the world would anyone know that? The doctors don't know it. When I hear those comments, I no longer have the freedom to say how I really feel."

"We've talked about some of the things we shouldn't say," I said. "What are some of the things we *should* say?"

Kelly's voice softened. "Well, through it all, you learn to be gentle with people even when they say the wrong thing. People want to be sensitive, but their fears get in the way. It's not always what you say, Deanna, but how much you care and how you feel inside. There have been times when I just needed someone to put a hand on my shoulder, or reach out and touch me, or bend down and give me a little kiss on the cheek. Just simple things. Sometimes there isn't anything you can say, but you can be there and listen, or you can make the other person feel comfortable by asking, 'Would you like to talk about it?'

"I went to see a young man whose mother had asked me to visit him. When I entered his room, I didn't know what to say. I started telling him about my travels, and I wanted to look away and out his window at the California sun. What do you say to a nineteen-year-old who's dying? I honestly couldn't think of one word, but I looked him in the eye, because I just couldn't look away, and finally said, 'Hey, listen. Are the drugs helping the pain?' He said, 'No, but your voice is. Just keep talking, if you would. It helps the pain go away. And will you hold me a moment before you go?' "

"Kelly, that's very special," I said, deeply moved.

"Well, I was a patient and he was a patient, and he was at a critical stage of his illness. I'll never forget what he said before I left. He said, 'Kelly, I'm really glad you're doing so well. I'm glad you're able to do what you're doing to help others. It makes me feel better that somebody can do it.' Beautiful, wasn't it? Just beautiful. You don't have any room for jealousy when you're dying. The bitterness that may have been there once is gone, all gone. The petty things don't matter. I guess the main message is to *express love now.* When you're with a dying patient, he may not have until tomorrow to hear the words 'I love you. You're not alone. We're going to see this through together. You are beautiful.' Give him the flowers now! I wrote a poem about that not long ago. Let me share it with you:

> Listen, sun! I want more than warmth from you.
> I need you to touch me, caress me,
> Dance about my fingertips and wrap my love
> In a blanket of today.
> One more sunrise . . .
> One more rainbow . . .
> One more day . . .
> Send the flowers before the sorrow.
> Do not wait until tomorrow.

A train whistle sounded in the distance, flying through the night like a silver ribbon, wrapping itself around us in the darkness. "You like train whistles, don't you, Kelly?" I asked.

"Yes. I can tell the difference between the freight trains and the nine-thirty Amtrak passenger trains. I hear train whistles all night long. Sometimes I don't know whether they're part of my dreams or whether they're reality, which is a good question. Where ends the dream and where begins reality when you're on drugs and it's night? Sometimes you doze for just a moment, and even while you're dozing, you're not completely asleep. You're in that land where the dead dreams go."

I was awakened early the next morning by the sound of the doorbell. Wanda and Kelly were still asleep upstairs, so I donned my housecoat and answered the door. It was a telegram from the president of the United States wishing Kelly a happy birthday.

Soon the sleeping household came to life. Kelly was pleased with the telegram and full of plans for the day. There were some cancer patients he wanted me to sing for before I began my long drive home. We would be visiting them later in the afternoon.

After breakfast I was given a tour of the house. Kelly's office was upstairs adjoining the bedroom. Lining the walls were front-page headlines about Make Today Count: "Learning to Live with Dying." "In the Certainty of Death, A New Outlook on Life." "The Cancer Man Faces the Toughest Break of Them All." "Dying Has Taught Him to Live."

"I met you long before you met me," I confessed, "under the terrible headline 'Facing Death He Finds Fame'."

"That's not so bad," Kelly chuckled. "You should have seen a California headline that read 'Dying Man Forms Organization of the Doomed.' Sounds cheerful, doesn't it?" One attribute Kelly had in abundance was a sense of humor. "You have to be able to laugh at yourself," he told me. "Otherwise, you might cry."

In his office and workroom, thousands of letters were stacked in cartons against the wall. "After a television appearance," he explained, "the mail sometimes runs to a hundred letters a day. Most are from others who have life-threatening illnesses. Many patients don't like the word *terminal.* They prefer the term *life-threatening* because we simply can't impose time limits on people. I've already outlived the doctors' deadlines, and I still have a lot of living to do. Many of the letter writers have questions, share problems and concerns, or just applaud the concepts of Make Today Count, which is a good philosophy for anyone." Kelly smiled wryly. "Some letters carry remedies for cancer—everything from skunk oil to carrot juice. One writer asked, 'Are you still alive?' "

The small room looked much like a newspaperman's office. Certificates and photographs lined the walls. The desk was stacked with papers arranged in an orderly fashion. Radio and stereo equipment stood against the wall opposite the desk. Beside them were shelves containing books and a prodigious array of medicine bottles full of pills potent enough to kill. "These medications have to be regulated very carefully," Kelly said. "If the cancer doesn't get you, the medicine will." The multicolored pills were designed to stop the cancer cells from spreading and help him through the difficult months of illness. He described the medicines and the incredible amount he had to consume daily just to keep going. He was becoming an expert on cancer research and treatment and was planning to write several books, including two to be titled "Make Today Count" and "Until Tomorrow Comes."

"I tell the doctors it's my body, and I want to know what is happening to it," Kelly said emphatically. "The biggest complaint we have from patients is not that they're being told too much. It's that they're not being told enough. In a way, I'm serving as an advocate between them and the medical profession. I guess I'm really two separate people living two different lives. I die among the living and live among the dying. Sometimes I get tired of these roles, and I feel much more comfortable here in my office, answering these letters. I don't have to put on a social front for anyone. Deanna, I think that if I could put together into one cry all the anguish and frustration expressed by the people who have contacted me, it would almost be heard around the world."

"I suppose that's why we first had such a negative reaction to the song 'Teach Me to Die,' " I said. "Shortly after I wrote the song, a nurse stopped me in the hall and asked me where I'd been. I told her I'd been asked to speak to a group of funeral directors. She looked startled and then asked, 'Deanna, why are you writing songs about death and singing for funeral directors? I always thought you were such a cheerful person!' People don't want to hear words like *death* and *dying.*"

Kelly was suddenly jovial. "Let's try to sing your song without using the word *die* in it," he said. "You begin."

"Teach me to expire," I quipped.

Kelly responded instantly. "Teach me to pass away."

"Teach me to terminate."

"Teach me to kick the bucket," Kelly returned quickly.

"Teach me to fly away," I said.

"Teach me to cross the River Styx," said Kelly.

By now we were both laughing heartily. "I have a great one!" he exclaimed. "Here's one you can't top: 'Teach me to jump in the chariot as it swings low.' " He paused, then asked in mock seriousness, "How can a chariot be 'sweet'?"

"You're right. I can't top that one." I laughed.

"Seriously," he said, "the reason your song meant so much to me is that I could listen to it and say, 'That song says just how I feel.' If the purpose of music is to reflect our feelings and experiences, why shouldn't we have a song about death? Not everyone in the world is walking around the streets healthy and strong."

"Kelly, how do you feel about music therapy in a hospital setting?" I asked.

"I think music is extremely valuable for anyone in a hospital, especially patients with life-threatening diseases. Some people may ask, 'How on earth can you play music for someone who's dying?' Well, we still have our likes and our dislikes. Why shouldn't we still like music? We need music while we're living, and we need music while we're dying. Sometimes we expect people to isolate themselves from us and die before they are dead, at least socially. We probably do the same thing with elderly people. Dying people are excluded from many so-called normal activities, and singing is one of those. Some professionals and even family members feel they have a right to determine what's best for a patient. Just because we're dying does not mean we've lost our feelings and sensitivities. No one is going to stop people who are well from going to a movie or a concert after they get off work. Some health-care professionals are sensitive and aware, but there are others who say, 'Hey, we've got rules to go by.' Maybe you're expected, as a dying patient, to respect the 'Quiet Please' signs, be very still, and just wait. But not me. I want to live until I die. And music helps me to live!"

Kelly picked up a pamphlet from his desk and handed it to me. "There are certain guidelines that can help make communication easier for both the patient and the family. I wrote these for Make Today Count."

I scanned the list of suggestions:

1. Talk about the illness. If it is cancer, call it cancer. Don't try to make life normal again by trying to hide what is wrong.

2. Accept death as part of life. It is.

3. Consider each day as another day of life, a gift from God to be enjoyed as fully as possible, rather than another day closer to death.

4. Realize that life is never going to be perfect. It wasn't before and it won't be now.

5. Pray. Don't be ashamed or afraid. It isn't a sign of weakness. It is your strength.

6. Learn to live with your illness instead of considering yourself dying from it. We are all dying in some manner.

7. Put your friends and relatives at ease yourself. If you don't want pity, don't ask for it.

8. Make all practical arrangements for funerals, wills, etc., and make certain that your family understands them.

9. Set new goals. Realize your limitations. Sometimes the simple things of life become the most enjoyable.

10. Discuss problems with your family as they occur. Include the children, if possible. After all, your problem is not an individual one.

It was a wonderful day, filled with sunshine and laughter, made even better by visits to Kelly's friends. Cecil, an emaciated cancer patient, managed a weak smile when we arrived. Family members were sitting around his bedside. He sang with us and talked about all the memories the music brought back to him. Soon the entire family joined in the singing. By the time we left, they had changed from sad, depressed people who felt the gloom of impending death to smiling people enjoying together their loved one's last hours.

Then it was time for me to go home. The sun was moving toward the western horizon when I crossed the bridge from Iowa into Illinois. I parked the car and walked through the trees, across the cracked blocks of soil, and onto the wet, sandy beach for one more look at Kelly's river. Clouds billowed over the city of hills, and a long barge moved slowly along the river. A brisk breeze fanned the water, and gentle gray waves lapped at the shore. I soaked in the magic, then rescued some bright seashells from the sand and tucked them into my pocket.

Already, in my mind, I was writing a song that would one day be a memorial tribute for a friend whose words of wisdom would be etched forever in my heart:

I saw you look across the Mississippi
When evening stars hung silent in the sky.
I watched you search the corners of tomorrow
As you wondered when your time would come to die.
I heard your sounds of life the night we listened
To the echo of a lonely distant train.

Just a Memory Away

I wonder if you know how much I'll miss you
When I watch the Mississippi in the rain.
I wonder if you'll hear the songs I'm singing
And remember all those poems you used to say.
I can leave you knowing that you'll always be there,
For you're only just a memory away.

The gray waters of the Mississippi were winding toward the sea as my wind-tossed plane carried me over Iowa farmlands a few years later. My heart was heavy—and not just with sadness. I was becoming more and more aware of how much love Orville Kelly had brought into my life. And this was to be my last visit with him. He had lived eight years from the time of his diagnosis, to the amazement of the medical profession. Every major newspaper in the country had shared his long battle. Would they remember him now that the struggle was nearly over?

Two nights earlier I had finished a performance in Boston and was settling into my hotel room when Kelly called from Iowa City Hospital. His voice sounded far away. "Deanna, if ever I needed your music, I need it now. Would you mind getting your guitar and singing my favorite songs? I want to hear them once more."

I sat down on the floor, my guitar cradled in my arms, the phone tucked under my chin. Salty tears got in my way as I tried to sing "Bridge over Troubled Waters," "You're Only a Memory Away," and "Bobby McGee."

"I'm not doing very well at this," I whispered, almost unable to talk over the lump in my throat. "I promise I won't behave like this at the funeral. It's just that you're such a hard person to say good-bye to."

That night I hastily rearranged my flight schedule to include a stop in Iowa City before going on to give a workshop in another state. I found Kelly in a tiny hospital room, his face pale. Wanda hugged me. Dark shadows circled her eyes, and her slight form seemed paper thin in my arms. I wanted to give them the world, a cheery room filled with spring blossoms and a big picture window overlooking the Mississippi. The cramped room provided just enough space for me to pull up a chair next to Kelly's bed.

"We may be moving him soon to the hospital in Burlington," Wanda said. "We want him to have a room overlooking the river."

"I read the headlines not too long ago," Kelly smiled wanly. "They said, 'Cancer Man Steals Another Year of Life.' But all the time death was creeping up on me while I was looking the other way."

"You sure fooled the doctors," I reminded him. "Remember when they only gave you two years?"

"Yes," nodded Kelly, "and in that eight years all my dreams came true. It's not every man who can say that, you know."

"What were your dreams?" I asked.

"Mostly to leave the world a better place than I found it. I think we helped people to face life and death with honesty and courage, and not to be afraid. We gave hope to veterans who were exposed to radiation, as I was, during the war. We helped in the understanding of one of the world's most fearful illnesses. And maybe, most of all, we helped people to learn to love better."

"We're going to miss you out there," I said, full of sadness. "Things just won't be the same without you."

"Well, you'll have a lot of memories," Kelly said.

I smiled in the remembering as a thousand images flashed before my mind. "Yes, like the time Elisabeth and I sneaked up to your doorstep at midnight to wish you happy birthday with arms full of wilted roses that we carried through four states! Remember that donut cake I made you? I purposely put a no-burn candle in the middle so it wouldn't go out. But when you blew it out, it stayed out. I was so mad at that darned candle!"

Kelly chuckled. "I'll never forget that Make Today Count workshop in Chicago. Bill Gray was there from the National Institutes of Health. We had to use tablecloths for handkerchiefs because we were all crying and there were no tissues.

And how can I forget how we ended all those meetings by standing in a circle holding hands singing 'Should Auld Acquaintance Be Forgot'?"

"Then there was the time we went wading in the ocean in San Diego," I added. "That lady fell down in two feet of water and thought she was going to drown! I remember when we were walking in Crapo Park and you saw a plane going over the Mississippi. You looked up and said, 'I flew over that river countless times. How I loved it! When I can't do it anymore, Deanna, do it for me.' That is a promise I intend to keep! And do you remember the poem you wrote for Wanda that you always used to recite at our seminars, 'Love Will Never Go Away'? You shared the words as I sang softly in the background about the seasons."

"Oh, yes," Kelly said. He began to recite the verses by heart, and I saw a mist in Wanda's eyes.

Spring, and the land lies fresh green
Beneath a yellow sun.
We walked the land together, you and I,
And never knew what future days would bring.
Will you often think of me,
When flowers burst forth each year
And the earth begins to grow again?
Some say death is so final,
But my love for you can never die.
Just as the sun once warmed our hearts
Let this love touch you some night
When I am gone
And loneliness comes . . .
Before the dawn begins to scatter
Your dreams away.

Summer, and I never knew a bird
Could sing so sweet and clear
Until they told me I must leave you
For a while.
I never knew the sky could be so deep a blue
Until I knew I could not grow old with you.
But better to be loved by you

Than to have lived a million summers
And never known your love.
Together, let us, you and I,
Remember the days and nights for eternity.

Fall, and the earth begins to die,
And leaves turn golden-brown upon the trees.
Remember me, too, in autumn, for I will walk
with you
As of old, along a city sidewalk at evening-time,
Though I cannot hold you by the hand.

Winter, and perhaps someday there may be
Another fireplace, another room,
With crackling fire and fragrant smoke,
And turning, suddenly, we will be together,
And I will hear your laughter and touch your face,
And hold you close to me again.
But until then, if loneliness should seek you out,
Some winter night when snow is falling down,
Remember, though death has come to me,

Love will never go away.

I had supposed that Kelly would want only Wanda and me in the room when we sang his favorite songs for the last time. It would be an intimate moment for just the three of us. That supposition was short-lived, for Kelly's eyes suddenly lit up. "Listen, Deanna," he said, "there are several patients on this floor who are extremely ill. One of them is a sixteen-year-old boy who has leukemia. Before you start singing, let's see how many of them would fit into this room. And bring the family members. They need the music too."

So it was that Orville Kelly died as he lived, thinking of others. I memorized those moments as we sang to our standing-room-only audience. Just before I left to catch my flight, I hugged the big man from Burlington in a tearful farewell. He slipped a piece of white scratch paper into my hand, saying, "I want you to have this."

I walked out of the hospital and into the sunshine, where I read the words Kelly had scribbled hastily:

I watched a parade this morning
High up in the sky.
I watched it from my hospital window
As the clouds went marching by.
At once the trees applauded
And the birds sang merrily.
I watched a parade this morning
And it was just for me.

I tried to put my finger on the gift, but it was undefinable and without price. It was the gift of a man who shared his life with others and created something beautiful up to the last moment. Perhaps the secret could be found in the words Kelly had spoken years before: "Deanna, you can die until you die or you can live until you die. Maybe you're expected as a dying patient to lie still and just wait. But not me! I want to live until I die!"

6

Take My Hand

After I met Orville Kelly, my interest in music therapy for dying patients grew rapidly. I began to take note of the many ways music helped them respond more positively to their world by fulfilling emotional and spiritual needs. Music allowed them to acknowledge and accept their feelings of sadness as well as joy, promoting emotional freedom. It created a bridge of communication between patients, staff, and family members and added a feeling of normalcy to the patients' lives. It helped them to recall events in their lives that were meaningful and to establish and maintain social relationships. Music gave them the feeling they were loved.

As I shared personal musical experiences, patients with life-threatening illnesses became my mentors, teaching me how to live in a way I had never before experienced. When I was able to grant their special requests, they began to give me a new awareness of what it means to be alive. Just as Kelly's wish to see one more snowflake was a simple one, so were most of the patients' wishes.

Bessie, a remarkable woman who was dying from complications of diabetes, had for many years sung with her daughter Ruth for clubs and church groups. One of her greatest wishes was to sing with her daughter one more time. Vickie and I arranged to go to the hospital on a Saturday when Ruth and other family members could be there. Knowing it would be a special event, I brought along my tape recorder.

As Bessie and her dark-haired daughter began to sing, their voices blended together in an unusual harmony, filling the room with some of the sweetest sounds I had heard in a long time. Bessie died the following Monday.

Several months later I sent Bessie's daughter a copy of the tape we had made in the hospital. Soon afterwards I received a letter from her. "I can't thank you enough for that wonderful tape you sent me," she wrote. "Words can't express what I felt when I heard my mom singing, laughing, and talking again. I have played it over and over. The first time I played it, it was very touching and I cried all afternoon. How I do love my mom! How very precious she was and still is to me. I think your work must be very rewarding—to be able to comfort people who are dying. Because of your songs, and my dear mother's attitude toward life and death, when my time comes to walk down the lane of death, I will be able to do it better. I know you meant a great deal to Mom, and she loved you dearly. I will never forget you."

One afternoon I sat by Ginny Berg's bedside, and she began to share how difficult it was to be a mother of two preschool boys and not be able to live to see them grow to manhood. Ginny lived in a small Illinois farming community. Her wide, dark eyes sparkled from her thin face, and she was always immaculate. After a diagnosis of cancer, chemotherapy treatments caused her marked hair loss. She compensated by wearing a natural-looking wig, and she looked lovely with her makeup and clothing.

Ginny derived her acceptance of her illness as well as her positive attitude from a lifetime of rich, meaningful living. "It's easier to bear, for both me and my family, if I keep my chin up," she would say. "I get down once in a while, of course, but then everybody does." She told me that if her husband ever married again, she hoped it would be to someone who would love her sons as she did.

Our roles could easily have been reversed. A mother of small boys myself, I identified closely with her. We were two young mothers sharing a burden too heavy to be carried alone. I remember Ginny in a special way because she was the first patient I cried with. Our tears were more like a gift to each other. She told me one day that I was the first person in the hospital who had cried with her.

One day, when I was visiting Ginny in her hospital room, she asked me a puzzling question. "Why me, Deanna?" The question is a natural one, especially for terminally ill patients who are angry or bitter. But Ginny didn't sound bitter.

"What do you mean?" I asked, wanting to be sure I understood.

"I was just wondering," she responded softly, "why God loves me so much. People have been so good to me, and they have done so much for my family. There are many critically ill patients in this hospital. I was just wondering why I'm being cared for in such a special way."

Ginny went into remission and, for a time, was able to return to the warmth of her family. I did not see her for a long time, but because of her I was more aware than I had ever been of the puffy white clouds above me and of the hugs of my little boys. I wanted to say it with a song, so I wrote "Take My Hand" for Ginny. The only problem was that I was still a bit shy about letting patients know how much I knew, and I had never sung this song personally for Ginny or let her know it was written for her.

Shortly before Christmas, when the branches of the trees were loaded with snow, a nurse told me Ginny was back in the hospital and wanted to see me. I maneuvered Sylvia in her wheelchair toward the nearly deserted wing where Ginny had been taken because of crowded conditions in other parts of the hospital. Sylvia was the new president of the women's auxiliary in our church. Because Vickie was transferring to another hospital, I thought it a good idea to enlist Sylvia's help. Her legs had been paralyzed with polio as a child of five, but otherwise she was a healthy, active wife and the mother of three fine children. Her voice must have been born in heaven because I had never heard an earthly voice like it, and I knew the patients would love it as much as I. She had consented to come for half a day as I had at first, and now was involved as deeply as I. And she had enrolled with me as a student at Illinois State University, where we were taking music therapy classes together.

When Sylvia and I entered the hospital room, I was startled by Ginny's appearance. Her condition had obviously deteriorated since the last time I saw her. She was no longer wearing her attractively styled wig, had no makeup on, and was dressed in a simple, white hospital gown. Even though cancer had robbed her body of its vitality, her face was unmistakably lovely, her large brown eyes clear as ever. The light within was still glowing.

"Aha!" she exclaimed. "Now you see me as I *really* am!"

"Ginny, you're *beautiful* as you really are," I said with conviction. She had never looked more beautiful to me than she was that afternoon.

"Am I glad you're here," she said with a sigh of relief. "Some of my friends who come to visit are becoming more uncomfortable. I make people nervous. They don't want to talk about what's happening to me, so they talk about the flowers or look out the window. If I can accept it, why can't they?"

Her comment reminded me of my own failure to communicate openly with my father when he was dying. I was determined not to regret my mistake, but to use it as teacher.

"How's your family doing?" asked Sylvia.

"My mom's pretty strong, but it really tears my dad up. It hurts me to see him like that. My husband, Ken, and I have been very close. I think we've done more living in the past six months than in all the years we've been married. I still worry about the boys."

"What's happening with *you,* Ginny?" I asked directly.

"My doctor wants me to go to Chicago for special treatments, but unless he can guarantee some kind of improvement, I don't want to go. There's no sense prolonging my life if it means I have to be away from my family. It just wouldn't be worth it. It would be terrible for me if I had to die away from everyone I know and love."

"I think that's a good decision," I affirmed. "Sometimes you can find eternity in only moments together."

Ginny agreed. "When you begin counting the moments, the quality of time you spend with your family becomes more important than the quantity. I know there's not much time left. I'm out of remission, and I don't think there's much anyone can do about it."

"I wish I could do something, Ginny," I said with all the feeling of a prize fighter wanting to go one more round. "We love you so much!"

"You know how much I love you, too," Ginny said, "but I've learned to look at both sides of this. It's easier to cope with that way. I guess there's still some hope. They brought my liver down once, and I wonder if they could do it again. But sometimes I get tired. I get so tired of dying! I ask myself, 'What will I do if they tell me this?' or 'What will I do if they ask me the opposite?' I think out ahead of time what I'll do, so that I'll be able to meet it calmly. I know I have to do this. No one else can do it for me. I've come to know that living and dying are part of each other. Dying is a part of life. People who have never experienced pain or sickness don't understand how I can feel that way, but I do."

She looked out the window at the snow coming down in big flakes. "It's almost Christmas," she mused. "I wonder if I'll be here to spend one more Christmas with my family. That's the hardest part, you know. When the people you love get all upset." She reached out and covered my hand with hers. "I went to a program you did in my community some time ago. You didn't know I was there. I just sat in the back and listened. At that program, you sang a song you had written about dying. That song really touched me. There were so many of my feelings in that song. Will you sing it for me now?"

As I sang "Teach Me to Die" again, I thought of the song I had written for Ginny. I felt a bit foolish that I had not shared it with her sooner. What if she died never knowing she had a song of her own?

"Ginny, I've written a song just for you," I confided. "I don't know why I've never sung it for you. I was sort of afraid, I guess. I just thought of all your feelings and the things you love, and I tried to put those feelings into a song. It's called 'Take My Hand.' " I sang the words gently.

Take my hand and walk a while with me.
Take my hand and talk a while with me.

Just yesterday my strong arms held my tiny infant son,
And yesterday my hands could work—my two strong legs could run.
I was the one with head held high and sunlight in my hair,
Running down the meadow lane, climbing up the stair.

Take my hand and share with me my fears.
Take my hand and let me see your tears.

Please don't forget to lift your head—
Don't let the clouds go by
Before you see the forms and shapes
They make against the sky.
Please take good care of all the things
I've treasured day by day—
Sunlit crowns on mountaintops,
Rows of new-mown hay.

Take my hand and walk a while with me.
Take my hand and talk a while with me.
Take my hand. You will see the wonders
Of the world in me.

Ginny's eyes were brimming with tears when I finished, but she was smiling. "That song is the most beautiful Christmas present I've ever received. Do you think it will go on helping others even after I'm gone? That way a part of me can just keep going."

"Your song and your love will touch many lives," I promised.

Just then I noticed a nurse closing the door to Ginny's room. Since we were on a deserted wing, I knew the songs were not bothering other patients. I excused myself and walked to the nurses' station. "I noticed the door being closed to Ginny's room," I said. "Is there a problem?"

"Not for us," said the nurse, "but one of our physicians was on the unit, and he overheard the words to some of the songs you were singing in Ginny's room. He expressed the concern that your songs were depressing the patient, so we thought it might be a good idea to close the door."

I rejoined Ginny and shared the conversation with her. "He thought we might be depressing you," I said, smiling.

Ginny sat up straight, and her eyes flashed as she said indignantly, "How does he know? He's never died before!"

We had a good laugh together. I hugged Ginny, then looked deep into her eyes. "I hope you're able to go home for Christmas. I just want you to know that because of you, I'm not so afraid."

Ginny did go home for Christmas—to the One whose birth we celebrated.

Not all our patients faced their illnesses with the same inner peace and equanimity as Ginny, and learning to understand and help them was a challenge. Some patients who were still lingering in denial or self-imposed exile were not ready to hear songs about death, such as "Teach Me to Die." To them I tried to sing only songs they loved and related to comfortably.

In any case there were risks to be taken, and I found that the best teacher was experience. When there was doubt about whether patients were ready to hear songs about their own confrontation with life-threatening illnesses, I sometimes left a tape in their rooms to give them the opportunity to listen to the songs privately. I could then discover their readiness more quickly from their reaction to the songs they chose to talk about.

One nurse gave a tape of "Peacebird" to a sixteen-year-old boy who was dying of leukemia. He left a note, which his family read after his death, explaining that he wanted them to remember him whenever they heard "Teach Me to Die" and "Put My Memory in Your Pocket." The family later wrote to the Franciscan Communications Center expressing their appreciation and asking if they could obtain copies of the album because of what the songs had meant to their son.

One day as I was approaching the room of a patient on the second floor, a nurse stopped me in the hallway just outside his door. "I've just come from his room, and I think it might not be helpful to sing to this patient," she cautioned. "In any case, I don't believe he would allow you to sing to him even if you offered."

"What's the problem?" I asked.

"He has terminal C.A. [cancer] and is one of the most difficult patients we've had on this floor. He has been extremely rude to the staff and to his visitors, and we don't know quite how to help him. He complains that we never answer his call button on time, that the food is lousy, and that the doctors are just keeping him here to get his money. But I guess I'll have to leave the decision up to you."

Her words registered slowly, with all the real and imagined fears that accompanied them. Ginny had been so easy to relate to, so open. What if I did more harm than good for this patient? I decided to take the risk. Ignoring all thoughts of failure, I entered his room. The curtains were drawn, and the room was dark, providing only minimal light. The patient appeared to be in his fifties. He had the weathered skin of a farmer, and a gray stubble was visible on his chin. His thin arms lay straight at his sides. A few cheerless cards stood on his dresser.

I was afraid of this man—afraid he would want to shut me out too, and afraid he would not allow me to walk with him for even a few moments down the dimly lit corridors of a fading life. I summoned all my courage and said, "My name is Deanna Edwards. I am a volunteer here in the hospital, and I'm wondering if you'd like a song today."

With an empty look in his eyes, he said icily, "No. I don't want a song. Now get out of this room and leave me alone."

Even though I had been forewarned, I was stung by his flat refusal. I wanted desperately to turn and run out the door. If patients refused a song because they were too sleepy, engrossed in a good television program, or visiting with relatives, making a gracious exit was not so difficult. But this time I could not move. Why on earth, I wondered, were my feet glued so firmly to the floor? As I felt my pride crumble in pieces around my feet, my intuition told me that if I walked out at that moment, I would be sentencing the patient to a prison of isolation. Then I began to doubt again: the door to his heart was one he definitely did not intend to open.

"May I sing just a short song?" I pressed, confident that a short song might be tolerated more easily than a long one. "It will only take a moment, and then I'll leave."

He seemed surprised that his verbal onslaught had not frightened me away. "One song," he said gruffly, as if he sensed it would be the only way to get rid of me.

"You Are My Sunshine" was the only short song I could think of at that moment. The words almost tumbled over each other. I felt a bit ridiculous singing a song about sunshine to a man who obviously saw so little of it in his world. Then his eyes met mine for the first time. It was like watching ice melt on a hot summer day.

When I finished, he asked a straightforward question: "Do you happen to know the song 'Home on the Range'? "

Thank you, God, I prayed silently. What if he had asked for a song I hadn't known? I had never been so glad to sing a request. No encore on a lighted stage and no cheering audience could have thrilled me more. I had sung the song hundreds of times, but in that darkened room, "Home on the Range" took on new meaning, even though the words "where seldom is heard a discouraging word" didn't seem to fit the circumstances.

As I sang, the man's thoughts appeared to be swimming through the leafy greens and sunny yellows of unforgotten days. When I finished, his voice was rich with remembering. "Do you want to know why I like that song?"

I could hear the echo of Dick Obershaw's words in Richmond: "Sometimes guitars can build walls instead of bridges." It was time to put the guitar away and pull the chair up close beside the patient's bed, to let go of the performance and listen to him. The music had helped to build the bridge. Now it was time for me to walk across it.

"I used to own a cattle ranch in Montana," he said, with the voice of a man who had suddenly found himself surrounded by a friendly, familiar landscape. "You should have seen it. I think it was the most beautiful ranch in the state. I can still smell the cattle and hear their sounds as we rounded them up at dusk. I used to sing that old song as I rode my favorite horse across the range. My voice didn't sound like much, but out there in the middle of God's country it didn't seem to matter. I can still remember the feeling of the wind on my face and the sun on my back. That's where I wanted to die, with my boots on, like a man. And here I am in this obscure hospital in Illinois, and I don't even know how I got here."

He lowered his voice. "I'll tell you something I haven't told anybody else," he confided. "I'm going to die very soon. They're going to wheel me out of here on a cart, and that's not my idea of dignity."

I felt impotent in the face of his struggle, but I did the one thing I hoped I could do for him. "I would want to be at home too, if I were you," I told him. "I can't take you back to that cattle ranch, but I can promise you one thing. If I ever have the opportunity to go to Montana, I'll take you in my heart. When I get there, I'll look for your cattle ranch. And when I find it, I'll think of you."

His calloused hand reached out to mine. "Would you really do that for me?" he asked. "That would mean more to me than I can tell you."

I don't remember how long we talked in the dim light of his room, but there was a touch of "forever" in those moments. When it was time for me to go, he reached out both his hands and grabbed mine urgently. He asked me two questions I knew I would never forget: "Do you have to go now? When are you coming back?"

I left his room thinking how sad it would have been had he died with the words *hostile* and *depressed* on a hospital chart, never having had a chance to share how he felt about his cattle ranch in Montana. He died a few days later. He was to be forever a part of my heart, and I hadn't even learned his name.

A few months later, a call came from the Montana Nurses Association asking me to give a workshop. I was happy for the opportunity to keep a promise.

I was flying over the state of Montana when my eyes filled with tears. I had been looking out the window and down upon ridges of blue hills. I don't really know where the man's cattle ranch was, but I felt, in a symbolic way, that I saw it. And I remembered him.

With the loss of home comes a loss of personal identity. When the only home a patient has left is the home that lives deep within the heart, we must find ways to bring those memories alive. We can transport a patient on the wings of a song to another time and place, back to that familiar landscape of home. It was wonderful to help patients take that musical journey into the human heart. Those experiences inspired me to write a song titled "Music Brings My Heart Back Home."

Weeds are growing in the meadow
Where the grass grew fresh and green,
And my home is only standing in my mind.
When I see you there before me
And I hear the songs you sing,
All those melodies turn back the hands of time.

There were cobwebs in the corners,
And the dust from yesterdays
Covered up the dreams I left there long ago.
You brought hope and understanding

And the strength to carry on
When you sang those loving songs I used to know.

I can hear the sounds of laughter!
I can feel the joy we knew!
All my memories come alive through gentle songs.
They bring back the faded pictures
And the colors in my life.
Music bring my heart back home where it belongs!

Some of the patients who had life-threatening illnesses tried to mask their feelings behind an air of indifference, especially the male patients. In our society men do not seem to feel as free as women to show their emotions openly, so they have a stronger tendency to feign indifference.

One day I entered the room of a patient who had been lying flat on his back. When he saw me, he raised up on his pillows.

"I'm a volunteer here at Mennonite Hospital," I greeted him, "and I wonder if you'd like a song today."

The gray-black hair was brushed back from the man's face, and he was wearing rumpled, brown-checked pajamas. Rows of get-well cards hung from the ceiling to the floor. The windowsill was crowded with plants and flowers. "Didn't I see you and another lady on closed-circuit television this morning?" he asked.

"Yes, my singing partner and I have been providing the inspirational music for the chaplains' closed-circuit television programs," I explained. "It gives the patients an opportunity to hear a good message as well as a chance to get to know our chaplains and other staff members."

"Well, I really enjoyed your music," he said. "Sing anything you like. I'm not particular."

After I sang a couple of up-tempo country songs, he interjected a grim announcement. "I have cancer."

"Where is the cancer?" I asked.

"All over in here," he said, rubbing his abdomen. "Six weeks ago I read an article in the Washington *Post* about cancer of the colon. I said to myself, 'I have all those symptoms.' I went immediately to the doctor. He didn't seem to know what was going on, so I went to another doctor. He knew immediately. The cancer had been growing fast, like a mushroom. The doctor said there was nothing the medical profession could do. There was too much cancer to remove surgically, so there's not going to be any surgery."

"How difficult for you," I said softly.

"Well, I don't feel too bad," he said almost lightly. "We all have to die sometime. Some die sooner and some later. I guess it's just sooner for me." He continued to speak casually about the cancellation of his life, as if it were the cancellation of a local football game. "The problem is . . ." His voice trailed away.

"What is the problem?"

"Well . . . I have a thirteen-year-old son who needs me. The others are older and on their own. My son will need me to help put him through college. I put my other kids through. One is married, living in San Francisco. But the money! I used to spend money like it was going out of style! I thought I was going to live forever, so I didn't save as much as I should have. If I had it to do again, we'd move to Texas. I had two job offers there, but friends said it was too hot. And it's too *humid* here."

"How is your wife responding to this?"

"She should be here any time now," he said, glancing at the door. "Actually," he added, lowering his voice, "my *wife* is my biggest problem right now. She is aware of my condition, but she denies there's anything seriously wrong with me. I've been sick before, and I've always gotten well. She thinks I'm going to get well this time. I don't know how to tell my wife that I'm dying. I've tried, but she won't talk about it. Our thirteen-year-old doesn't know how sick I am either. They think I have another ten years. I don't think I have more than seven months. That's not much time to do all I want to do. You know, sometimes my minister comes to see me, but he always wants to talk about heaven. I don't mind if he wants to talk about heaven, but that's not where my

mind is right now. I just want to get out of this hospital and do something!"

"What do you want to do?" I asked. "Take a trip?"

"We did take a trip," he said, his eyes lighting up. "We went to Hawaii. That's the most beautiful place I've ever seen. You get there and you ask, 'Am I in heaven?' "

A nurse appeared in the doorway, smiled, and asked how he was.

"Where's my watermelon?" he demanded. "You promised to smuggle in a watermelon. You know how much I've been wanting one."

"I didn't dare," she apologized, "but maybe I could still get you one. We could squeeze out the juice and give that to you."

"To heck with the juice," he snorted. "I want a real watermelon so I can sink my teeth into it and spit the seeds up at the ceiling."

"I'll see what I can do," she said, laughing.

He chuckled as she left the room. "I hear the nurses are

even taking karate lessons now," he said. "That's so they can handle patients like me." He pointed proudly to the many cards covering the wall. "Look at all those," he said. "My wife even took some with her. The cleaning lady was always knocking them off the dresser, so I said, 'Take those cards home!' "

I surveyed the vast array with admiration. "There must be many people out there who care a great deal about what happens to you."

He was half-embarrassed, but determined to maintain the front that masked his deepest feelings. "They probably sent the cards because they want some money. I haven't paid all my bills. I might as well send them each twenty dollars and get them off my back."

"I wonder if I could sneak in a watermelon," I said mischievously.

"It's not just the diet they put me on," he commented. "You should taste the tea they give you here. They send up water with a little bag so you can make your own. By the time it gets here, the water is cold and the bag just floats around on top. I don't mind simmered, home-cooked tea—the mint kind like my grandmother used to make—but after two weeks of the other kind, I raised the roof. Now they've changed my diet a bit."

He stopped talking for a moment and gazed out the window at the clear sky. "You know, I wish I'd been more religious. I never was much of a churchgoer. But you can bet I'm searching for God now. There's got to be something more out there. Now I read the scriptures a lot. And I'm in touch with God." He smiled. "I've even sent Him a few cards."

"I'll bet you sent them Special Delivery," I said, laughing. The patient was being so open, so casual. I had the feeling a great many emotions had been locked tightly inside him since his diagnosis. I decided to risk again. "I've written a song about dying," I said. "I'm wondering if it would be okay if I sing it to you."

"Certainly," he said. "If I don't like it, I'll tell you."

There was no doubt in my mind that he would tell me just that. As I sang the first verse and moved into the chorus, his mask of indifference melted away in tears.

> Teach me to die. Hold onto my hand.
> I have so many questions—things I don't understand.
> Teach me to die. Give all you can give.
> If you'll teach me of dying, I will teach you to live.

Never before in my work had I experienced such a dramatic exchange of nonverbal communication. With his eyes he was telling me, *Yes, I really do care that I am dying. It matters. I want to learn how to do this, but I want to live, too.*

"Thank you," he said in a half-whisper. "That was beautiful. That song says how I feel."

"I thought I heard singing," came a voice from the doorway. The patient's wife entered the room. When she saw her husband's face streaked with tears, she ran to the side of his bed, grabbed a tissue from his nightstand, and began to wipe away his tears.

"Frank, I've never seen you cry before!" she exclaimed. "Why in the world are you crying now?" She looked at me angrily. "What are you doing to my husband?"

Frank did not refuse his wife the opportunity to dry his face, but waited patiently until she had finished. "I was touched by a very special song," he explained to her. "Can't you understand that sometimes I need to be able to cry? It's a release." He spoke as if he were pleading with her to come to terms with the reality of what was happening to him.

She turned to me with a forced smile—a look of confusion. "He never cries about anything." She had, perhaps for the first time, moved a little closer to the awareness that her husband was gravely ill.

I wanted to help her and to make her feel more at ease. I sensed a need for a cheerful, up-tempo song to help her cope with her new awareness. When we take people into an intimate musical valley of their feelings, we realize it is important to sing songs before leaving that will lift them up again.

"Do you like to get up early?" I asked.

"Not me," she said, relieved that the conversation had moved to a more comfortable area. "I don't really get going until about eleven at night. Then it's almost impossible for me to get out of bed in the morning."

"You should see her at night," the patient said with unfeigned affection. "There I am, drifting in and out of sleep, and I hear her banging around the house, hanging her drapes or painting the walls at two A.M. Then she complains that she can't get up to make my breakfast."

"So, I've found a kindred spirit!" I exclaimed. "It takes me an hour to open my eyes, and then I can't find my slippers. I stagger around for another hour before I'm able to function like a normal human being." I laughed. "I wrote a special song for people like us about getting up in the morning. Would you like to hear it?"

She nodded, and I began my unique rendition of "Brand New World":

When you wake up in the morning
To the old alarm clock ringing,
And only one wool slipper can be found,
Do you jump back into bed,
Throw the covers on your head,
Wishing that the night was still around?

Greet the shining dawn that's breaking,
Check the progress you are making,
Don't think about what happened yesterday.
Take no worry for tomorrow
With its happiness or sorrow.
There's too much life to live today!

It's a brand new world every morning,
Golden hours that will never come again.
It's another special day
And the love you give away
Will be measured by the broken hearts you mend!

We were quiet for a few moments after I finished the song. Then the wife commented, "Sometimes we do think of the hours we have wasted. We wish we could turn the clock back, but we can't."

"But, honey, we have today," her husband reminded her. "And we've shared so many good times and happy memories. Remember our trip to Hawaii? We had to get away from all the tourists and into the surrounding islands so we could find our own little cottage with the dirt road and the flowers!"

Before we said good-bye, I sang the Hawaiian song "Aloha Oe": "One fond embrace until we meet again . . ." They cried together as I sang.

I learned through this experience that our concern cannot revolve only around the patient. Often, family members require as much help and counseling as the patient. They must be cared for together. All patients, even though they need truth and openness, also need to maintain hope. Their hope may change from "I hope I can get well and go home" to "I hope I can be with my family for a few more months" to "I hope my children will be all right after I am gone." In the case of the patient for whom I had just sung, his hope was that his wife would come to grips with his illness and that they could begin to communicate honestly and live fully every day they had left together.

Because of this and many other unforgettable experiences with the terminally ill, my interest in music therapy for dying patients was increasing. But I found literature on the subject scarce. I began to study a pilot program that had been started by a cancer patient at Roswell Park Memorial Institute in Buffalo, New York. Then an invitation to appear at Forbes Health System in Pittsburgh, Pennsylvania, led to a meeting with other music therapists who were working in a hospital setting. I became aware of Jack Stukki's work at Colorado State Hospital in Pueblo, as well as the work of Susan Munro, a Registered Music Therapist (RMT), at Royal Victoria Hospital in Montreal, Canada, and Ruth Bright, an RMT from Australia.

My workshop opportunities were increasing. I was asked

to share my music at the national convention for the American Health Care Association, and that meeting led to numerous state conventions for health-care professionals around the country.

I began to encourage health-care administrators to hire registered music therapists as part of the staff, and encouraged facilities to build music carts that could be wheeled from room to room. At a nursing home in Minnesota, an administrator proudly showed me a cart he had designed and built after he heard my suggestion at a state convention. It was made of wood and had wheels and compartments designed to provide a wide variety of music. On the left side was a built-in record player and a compartment to store albums. On the right side was a built-in tape recorder and a drawer for the storage of cassette tapes. There was also a compartment for holding rhythm instruments that residents could play while listening to instrumental tapes.

I discovered that even family members could bring music to their loved ones with the aid of a cassette player. After a visit to some of the southern states, I received a memorable letter from a workshop participant, JoAnne Levin of Raleigh, North Carolina:

> Dear Deanna,
>
> This is a very informal note. I only met you once but feel that I know you well. I attended your presentation in Raleigh, North Carolina, several weeks ago on the recommendation of a friend who had heard you during your spring tour. I really had no preparation for the event and, over the course of the three hours, developed an emotional involvement that I shall never forget.
>
> My mother was a patient that day at Rex, dying of terminal brain cancer. After taking care of her at home for a year, I had exhausted most of my internal resources for coping and was praying that somehow I could struggle, as she was struggling, through the final days. Being a nurse in an intensive care unit, I have dealt with death many times, but somehow the loss of a mother is

a different experience altogether. A mother's love can never be equaled.

From your selection of songs I particularly related to "Walk in the World for Me" and "My Mother's Hands," so I chose to share these with my mother. For several days at my mother's bedside, these songs were my constant inspiration and my mother's "tranquilizer" when all else failed. For the last hour of her life I played the songs over and over again. In spite of my terrible head cold and shaky voice, I sang along with you. The words were *my* words too, and as the last song ended on your tape, my mother took her last breath. It was such a beautiful experience, and I want to thank you for the most wonderful Christmas gift of all—my mother's peace. I am sending along a little ornament I made for your tree and hope that you and your family will have a joyous holiday season.

This was the beginning of my musical journey into the human heart and the dawning of an awareness that music can bring "home" to those who cannot go home. Indeed, music can have a profound influence on the long-term care residents in at least ten major ways. It can

1. Combat dehumanization by helping residents and patients feel wanted and needed.

2. Help alleviate fears of being admitted to a hospital or a long-term care facility, and of necessary medical procedures.

3. Help develop constructive recall and give life to the "home" that lives within each person.

4. Enhance social skills and the desire to be involved in a variety of activities.

5. Give opportunities to express affection.

6. Build bridges of communication between residents, patients, and staff members.

7. Provide sensory stimulation with opportunities to play instruments or feel the rhythm of a guitar or drum.

8. Provide motivation in physical therapy, exercise techniques, or wheelchair dancing activities.

9. Minimize and sometimes even alleviate pain through active participation.

10. Provide a stimulant for the withdrawn and the comatose.

Being there with sick and dying patients is a gift many can give at almost any time. Anyone who has a caring heart and a listening ear can qualify to help someone in need. This thought was well expressed by a friend of mine, A. Jann Davis, R.N., from Charles City, Iowa. She has lived with prolonged illness herself, and has written several books, including the award-winning *Listening and Responding*. She wrote the following poem, "Please See My Need."

Take time to hear my words;
Please know that I'm still here.
Outside I'm weak and sick and worn;
Inside my heart knows fear.
I have so much I want to say,
There's so much undone to do.
I don't want a world of cold machines.
I just want some time from you.

You check for fever, you check for pulse,
And then you're on your way.
Oh please, just sit and hold my hand
A few minutes. Can't you stay?

Skip my bath. Don't change the sheets.
Use this time instead.
Let me share the fears I know.
Please, sit here by my bed.

Inside I beg, but I can't ask.
Your time is yours to give.
So many need your help and care,
So many—who will live.

I've used up all the time I have,
I now await the day.
So, God, I pray You'll see my need.
Please, send someone who'll stay.

7

A Christmas Gift

It was Christmas Day. An icy wind blew a few of the last brown leaves across the frozen snowdrifts, leaving bare trees to cast a pattern against the cold blue sky. It felt good to be inside where it was warm and cozy, but I couldn't shake the feeling that I was needed at the hospital. I tried to ignore the feeling, but it wouldn't go away. I kept thinking that if I found it delightful to be at home with Cliff, the children, and soft Christmas lights, how lonely must be some of the patients who couldn't go home for Christmas for even a few minutes.

I called to Cliff, who was in the living room. "Honey, would it be all right with you if I go to the hospital for a while this afternoon?"

After a brief silence, he called back, "Deanna, do you feel you have to go today? Christmas is a family day. Couldn't you go tomorrow?"

I walked into the living room, and his eyes met mine. "Cliff, I don't know why. I just feel there's someone in the hospital today who needs me."

Cliff's voice softened as he sensed the urgency in my voice. "If you feel it's important, then you should go." He smiled. "Just don't be gone too long."

The hospital was quiet when I arrived, with only a few people on duty. A Christmas tree stood in the waiting room, its drooping branches tied with bright red bows. Most of the patients who were not seriously ill had been released so they could spend the day with their families, and I noticed many empty beds in the rooms as I walked down the hallway on the main floor.

I entered the elevator, wondering where I should go first, and, without thinking, pushed the third-floor button. Usually I began rounds in the eye-care unit on the second floor, but I decided to change my routine today. I felt instinctively that some Christmas songs were not appropriate in a hospital on Christmas Day, so I decided to avoid such songs as "I'll Be Home for Christmas" and "I'll Have a Blue Christmas Without You," songs that had a potential for depressing patients who could not go home.

Room 381, next to the nurses' station, is one I will never forget. It was dimly lit by the fading afternoon sun. Outlined against the window, a man sat on the edge of his bed smoking a cigarette. There was not a sign of Christmas anywhere in his room. No sprig of holly or bright ornament. No Christmas cards or gifts. The only possession he seemed to have in the world was his cigarette. I looked into his thin, gray face and judged him to be in his early sixties. The veins stood out above his temples, accentuated by his baldness. A white hospital gown was draped about his slight form.

The patient's face registered surprise and curiosity when I entered his room, and I could hear the unspoken question, *What are you doing here?*

"I'm a volunteer at the hospital," I said, "and I thought some of the patients would like to hear Christmas carols. Would you like to hear my favorite, 'Silent Night'?"

He listened with unfeigned interest as intently as I had ever seen a patient listen. When I finished the song, his eyes narrowed and he said, "Do you happen to know the song 'I'll Be Loving You Always'?"

If he had been a physician writing his own prescription, the song could not have been a better one. The impact of the words was strikingly real: "I'll be loving you . . . not for just an hour, not for just a day, not for just a year, but always." It was a song of commitment that reflected not just this man's need but the need of all of us to be loved and cared for. As

I sang the promise, I became a bit uncomfortable. *What if he expects me to love him?* I thought.

"I failed this time, but I won't fail next time," he muttered when I finished the song. The words fell like stones in the silence.

"What do you mean, Paul?" I asked. I had caught a glimpse of his name plate above the bed.

"I failed to take my life," he said simply. "Like I said, the next time I try, I won't fail."

My heart jumped, and I was speechless for a long moment. I had surmounted all the other hurdles—first the long- and short-term care patients, then the dying patients. But Paul was the first person I had met who had been admitted for attempted suicide. What could I say to him? Intuition told me it would be more important to listen than to talk. I asked only a simple question to open the door: "Why do you want to die?"

He promptly answered my question with a question: "Why should I want to live? I haven't received a card, letter, or phone call from anyone for almost twenty-two months. If I should die tomorrow, no one would cry. I'm not sure anyone would even show up for the funeral."

"Don't you have a family?" I asked, horrified that anyone could be so alone in the world.

"My only son . . ." He hesitated a moment. "My only son was killed in Vietnam. I haven't been able to locate my daughter-in-law and my four grandchildren. The oldest would be seventeen or eighteen by now. I've written to them, but I always receive the same response—'Moved. Left no forwarding address.' So many times I've wondered what they're doing, and if they're all right."

Paul's eyes suddenly lit up. "You know, life wasn't always this way. There was a time when I was loved. Sometimes those days get very fuzzy in my mind, but music brings the memories back."

Suddenly I remembered the words of a resident I had met in a nursing home in Alabama: "Music: we love it for what it helps us to remember and for what it makes us forget."

"There's a song my Dad and I used to sing when we attended a little country church in the Midwest," Paul continued. "Do you happen to know 'How Great Thou Art'?" He stuttered slightly and crushed the remainder of his cigarette in a nearby ashtray.

I strummed the guitar, softly at first, and began to sing. "Oh, Lord, my God, when I in awesome wonder . . ." The chorus was stronger: "Then sings my soul, my Savior God to Thee . . ." A warm, mellow voice joined mine. Paul was singing with me. All traces of stuttering had disappeared. His voice was clear and true. Many patients with speech impairments who could not remember how to speak in a sentence could sing their favorite songs all the way through. The remarkable thing about Paul was the almost professional quality of his voice.

"You have a beautiful voice, Paul!" I exclaimed when we finished, feeling as if I had just discovered a buried treasure. "Are you a musician?"

"Of course I'm a musician," he said emphatically, as if to add, "Can't you tell one when you hear one?" "When I was not much more than a kid, I was playing solo trumpet, and I joined a band. I could do anything—hit C above high C without hardly touching the mouthpiece. I could really get up there—bust light bulbs from the vibrations. Sometimes I played that trumpet till it was white hot and still heating."

"If you played as well as you sing, that must have been some playing," I commented.

"Ah," he continued modestly, "I sound like an old crow. But I do have a good whiskey tenor." He chuckled to himself. Then he looked at my guitar. "I've been around a lot of hospitals, and I've never seen one of those before. I kind of like the idea."

"Since you're a musician, how long has it been since you've sung or played your trumpet?" I asked.

"I gave up playing long ago," he said. "I haven't really sung for about twenty years."

"You haven't sung for twenty years?" I asked, incredulous. "I can't go five minutes without singing. How did you pull off an absence of twenty years?"

"Well, to tell you the truth, I haven't felt like singing. I've been alone for twenty-six years. In fact, the music brings back a lot of memories. Both my father and my mother loved music. It sort of brings back the good about the past and reminds me of a time when life was worth living. I wasn't always alone, you know. I had a beautiful family. But that was a long time ago."

He lit another cigarette. "I should get rid of these things," he said, looking disdainfully at the cigarette. "They're terrible for your health. The doctor says they're bad for my circulation. Living a long life doesn't mean that much to me, so I guess I've never tried to stop smoking. It's the same with alcohol. I graduated from high school when I was eighteen years old. After that, I started driving a cab. It was then that I was introduced to alcohol and got to know every bootlegger in the city of Minneapolis. I tried drugs too, but I didn't like the after-effects.

"Things went from bad to worse, and I lost one job after another. That's when I joined a band again and started playing solo trumpet. I was married when I was twenty-one. Then I joined the National Guard. I was in the medical corps when Dad died, and I got my ticket home. I was having so many drinking problems that my wife was going to leave me. Well, I talked her into staying and giving me another chance. We drove out to California to a town just this side of Los Angeles to look at a business that the two of us could run. We'd been in the restaurant business in Minneapolis, where we'd made a pretty good income, but I was drinking it up as fast as we were getting it in. On the way back from California, there was an accident. I didn't see the other car on the bridge until he was almost on us. My wife was killed. I don't know why I was saved. I used to pray every night that I wouldn't wake up in the morning, because I was so lonesome. I still pray that . . ."

It was Christmas Day, a day when most people were praying for safety, protection, and abundant life. Paul was praying for death. I had heard that the suicide rate soared during the holidays because the celebration of families accentuated the pain of those who were alone. But Paul was not a statistic yet, and I prayed he would not become one.

"Well, I really started hitting the bottle after that," he continued. "My son was staying with relatives by then, and for about a week I drank steadily. I never ate a meal. I drank anything that came along. I wasn't fussy, so long as I could get drunk and stay drunk. That's when I made my first suicide attempt. I took a box of sleeping tablets. Two or three days later I woke up in a hospital. I had had a long sleep, but I was still alive.

"About that time a cousin of mine who was a nurse talked me into taking an examination to become a psychiatric aide in a state mental institution. Such institutions were really short on help, she said. I passed the test with a high score and became an aide in charge of a ward at a state hospital. I'd been in the medical corps in the army and was the son of a doctor, so I guess it came natural for me. Then I had a stroke. Arthritis and circulation problems also began to set in, and I haven't been able to work since then.

"I moved into an old boardinghouse on the west side of town here in Bloomington, and on the twenty-first of December I decided again to end it with tranquilizers and alcohol. My landlady found me, and the next thing I knew I had a fleeting consciousness of someone shining a light in my eyes. I imagined I was in the emergency room—or in heaven. I didn't know for sure. I woke up in this room the next morning, clear-headed but a failure at suicide again. I can't do anything right."

Suddenly a wonderful thought hit me. "Sounds like you did okay when you were working in a hospital," I said casually. "Ever thought of volunteer work?"

"Not really," he said. "I've never done anything like that before."

"Every Thursday we have a sing-along downstairs in the Activity Therapy Department," I said carefully. "We sure could use a voice like yours. Why don't you try it for half a day?" I almost chuckled. I knew what half a day could lead to.

"Do you really need me?" he asked.

"Of course we need you," I retorted. "Why do you think I asked?"

"I still sound like an old crow," he said, "but I guess I'll try it." He tried to sound reluctant, but his words were shining with hope.

The afternoon sun had gone down and it was getting dark out. I knew there would be no more time to sing for other patients. But that was all right. I had come to the right room.

"Since you haven't had a letter for almost two years," I told him, "I'm going home to write you a long letter, and I'll even bring it to you in person. In the meantime, our volunteer supervisor will come by to talk with you."

I picked up my guitar and turned to leave. I had just reached the door when I heard Paul's voice from the stillness: "Jesus sent you here today, didn't He, for my Christmas present."

"Yes, Paul, I believe He did."

I knew that my commitment to Paul could not be a halfhearted one. If someone did not reach out to him now with genuine concern, he might not live to see another Christmas. But my new commitment was not just for Paul. I made a resolution that whenever possible, I would go to the hospital on Christmas Day to sing for the patients. There were doubtless other Pauls out there, waiting for someone to find them. By the time I got around to writing Paul's letter, a soft snow was beginning to fall and the wind whistled around the window in the study. It was a long letter, as I had promised, filled with cheery thoughts and poems. But the most important message came in the last line: "P.S.: I'll be loving you always."

The activity therapy room looked different when I walked into it the first Thursday after New Year's Day. The walls had the same colorful posters, and handmade gifts and pillows decorated the shelves. The same residents were sitting around the table, busily occupied. The big difference was Paul, sitting in the midst of them and grinning from ear to ear. I took off my coat, rubbed my hands to warm them up, and sat down beside him. He was almost bursting with things to tell me.

"Ever since you came into my room Christmas Day and got me to singing, things have been starting to click!" he exclaimed. "The volunteer supervisor came into my room last week and introduced herself. She talked to me for about thirty minutes and told me that as soon as I got out of the hospital, she had some papers for me to fill out. So when the doctor came by on rounds, I said, 'Doc, get me out of this hospital!' He looked at me like I was nuts. He said, 'Why?' I said, 'Volunteer service wants me to go to work.' He said, 'How about this noon. Would that be soon enough?' "

"That's fantastic, Paul!" I responded. "What are you doing in your new work as a volunteer?"

"Well, I help get residents down from the floors for activities, and I help take them back to their rooms after therapy. I don't take all of them—just my share, and I help get the wheelchairs down again for dinner. I'm tired. It hurts me to walk sometimes, but I don't feel much pain, because I feel like I'm helping somebody else. I used to feel so doggone sorry for myself, remembering what I used to do and what I couldn't do now. It's the thought of 'nothing' that drives people to suicide."

"Looks like you have a lot more to do now than 'nothing,' " I observed.

Paul grinned. "On the second floor there's a guy by the name of Louie. He got to cryin' the other day, and I got to talkin' with him, and he said, 'Paul, you talk like you've been around guys like me.' I said, 'I have, old buddy!' And it wasn't long before he stopped crying. He started talking—

said he was an old railroad man—and since I had worked on the railroad for a while, we had something in common to talk about.

"Just about that time, Harold, another resident, decided to come over from his room carrying two pairs of britches. He wanted the nurses to do some sewing on them. When he got to the nurses' station, he didn't know what to do. He forgot where his room was. He didn't get lost—his room did! When he started walking into one of the women's rooms, I started after him. I finally got him to his room, but it was quite amusing. Some of these elderly residents get so confused."

"Yes, but they know when people really care about them," I said.

Paul chuckled. "Half the time during the Rose Bowl parade on New Year's Day, some elderly lady wanted me to hold her hand."

"Did you hold her hand?" I teased.

"I sure did!" he exclaimed. "She just didn't want to be alone. She began to talk about her son. He has a print shop in one of those little towns around Bloomington, and she wanted to know if I knew him. Naturally I said I did—and I told her that he was doing a good business, even though I had never heard his name."

"But you told her you did to make her feel good," I interjected.

"Sure! It really made her happy." He smiled. "I don't know if I know how to give happiness, but I do know many of the conditions of patients and how to follow their behavior patterns. I guess my experience in the state hospital helped. I enjoy this volunteer work so much. It's a lot better than straight bedside nursing. You have more time for the residents."

"I believe you were really cut out for this kind of work, Paul," I said.

"Yes," he agreed. "And I'm going to have to start learning all the residents' names. I'm not getting a dime out of this, but it reminds me of the work I used to do, and I love it. The guys in my boardinghouse think I'm a darn fool because I come to the hospital every few days. I told them, 'I don't care what you think. It's occupying my mind and heart and keeping me busy.' "

Within a year's time Paul contributed seven hundred hours of service to the hospital. He loved all the work he was asked to do, but his favorite day in the week was Thursday, the day of our long-term care sing-along. After carefully choosing the songs he wanted to sing, he practiced them and then sang out with the confidence of a seasoned performer. He especially loved the old songs: "Let Me Call You Sweetheart," "Down by the River Side," and our favorite, "Ain't She Sweet." To the latter song, Paul would add embellishments like, "Ain't she sweet, oh, yeah! / See her comin' down the street, oh, man!" He made the song come alive for all of us. No one could sing it as he did.

Paul had tremendous empathy for those who were lonely and vulnerable. Whenever any of us were unable to come to the hospital because of illness, mysterious cards would appear in our mailboxes, always signed "Get well soon. We love and miss you. Donald Z. Duck." For a while, no one could figure out just who Donald Z. Duck was.

One day in the activity therapy room, Paul was busy helping a resident paint ceramics. "Have you ever heard of Donald Z. Duck?" I asked.

For a moment Paul registered surprise. His grin was sheepish. "How did you know it was me?"

"I had a feeling it was you," I said, smiling. "Why do you do that? Why do you always remember us with these funny notes and cards when we're not feeling well?"

"I remember what it's like to be forgotten," Paul explained. "You see mail come along in the hospital, and they pass it out but skip you. I just decided that's not going to happen to any of my friends."

"The next time you get sick, Paul, I'm going to send you a dozen cards," I promised.

He looked me straight in the eye and said, "I'd rather have *you.*"

There was still the problem of family. Staff members, residents, and volunteers in the hospital had become Paul's family, but the missing members were still on my mind. Sylvia and I had a birthday party for him and gave him an elaborately decorated cake inscribed "Happy Birthday, Donald Z. Duck." We had a special Christmas party for him in the unit his first Christmas with us, and invited him into our homes for dinner on occasion. But I knew he still yearned to be in touch with his daughter-in-law and four grandchildren.

After many long-distance calls and much searching, I still had not located them. I decided to write to one of the editors of the *National Enquirer* because I had heard they could find anybody anywhere. Not long afterward, I received a letter from Malcolm Balfour, an editor, telling me the family had been located and they sincerely hoped Paul would once more enjoy being part of a family.

I called Paul's family, full of excitement, only to learn that his son had not been killed in Vietnam. He was still very much alive. Due to past wounds, still unhealed, he had disowned his father. He told me he did not want to be in contact with Paul. Knowing the dangers of being judgmental, I inquired about the children, asking about their ages, their talents, and their progress in school. He was willing to tell me all about his children so I could take the news back to Paul. Bitter walls of memories between father and son would not be torn down easily.

When I returned to the hospital, I was not sure how much Paul would want me to know, so I revealed my information slowly. "Paul, we've finally located your family."

"Maybe my son was not killed after all," Paul said cautiously. "Maybe he was just a prisoner of war."

I knew from his statement that it was all right for me to know his son was still alive. I also knew it had been easier for him to admit the absence of his son than to admit the absence of his son's love, so I focused only on the grandchildren. I told him about their activities, what they looked like, and how well they were doing.

"Thank God they're all right," he said. "That's all any man would want to know."

It was the last time Paul ever talked about his family. After a year of volunteer service, he suffered a toe injury that failed to heal. He was hospitalized for some time, and then finally the difficult decision had to be made to amputate his leg. As we struggled through that painful experience together, Paul never once gave up. Sylvia's example was like a shining light to him. "If she can be an effective volunteer from a wheelchair, so can I," he said. "There are a lot of things I can do. I can still help with the activities, shave the male residents, and sing in our sing-along."

So every Thursday we piled Paul's and Sylvia's wheelchairs into the trunk of the car and drove to the hospital. Paul himself had to be moved to a long-term care facility in town because of the difficulty of living in the boardinghouse. Though his volunteer service was more limited, he continued to serve until circulation problems damaged his kidneys. He was readmitted to Mennonite Hospital with kidney failure, and to the same room where I had first found him.

Paul did not have to die alone. He was surrounded by people who loved him and appreciated all he had done to make life happier for them and for others. The last time I saw him, I was sitting at his bedside. My eyes red with tears he could not see because his eyes were swollen shut. The words he spoke, I have never forgotten.

"You know that Christmas Day you came into my room?" he said. "I'm so glad you came, because I didn't really want to die. I just wanted to learn to live. And I have. I've had two of the greatest years of my life. At first I figured you'd run out of my room when I told you why I was in the hospital. Most people think anyone who tries to commit suicide is nuts. But you didn't leave. You stayed and listened and played your guitar. When you walked out that door, every desire I had to drink—or to die—walked out with you. Because you loved and accepted me, I began to love and accept myself. Now I kind of like myself. You taught me to do that."

"No, Paul," I said. "You were the teacher. You taught us so much about living and loving."

He smiled wisely. "I didn't teach you a thing you didn't already know."

In that same bed, in room 381, Paul died a few days later. His wallet contained a faded piece of paper, a poem I had hurriedly written and given to him:

One day a stranger crossed my way
Upon the road of life.
He was tired of the stony path
And weary of the strife.
I had no gift of gold
Or wreath to give to him that day—
So I gave his heart a song to sing
As he went along life's way.

Snow covered all his cherished dreams
As he walked through life alone.
He seemed to have no special friends—
No home to call his own.
But God sent him a message clear:
He had a work to do.
Now he works, he gives, he laughs, he lives,
To strengthen me and you.

And even when discouragement
Makes other people sad,
Paul is there to cheer them up
And make their spirits glad.
He never stops to count the cost
Or think about the pain—
And when a friend has fallen down
He picks him up again.

We love you, Paul!

8

The Littlest Angel

On a frosty December afternoon, my son Steve and our friend, Doug, and I struggled through the crowds into Texas Stadium in Dallas. Football fans jostled each other good-naturedly, and I grabbed the hands of my two young companions.

Steve and I had arrived from Salt Lake City the evening before. He was the budding athlete in our family. There was a kind of magic in his eyes as he anticipated watching the Dallas Cowboys in person for the first time. Doug Turno, the little boy clutching my left hand, had been here before and had traveled all the way from Aiken, South Carolina, to watch the game with us. A veteran Cowboy fan, he never watched them play without his special good-luck charms tucked securely into his pocket—a worn rabbit's foot and a furry seal made in Alaska. He somehow felt the charms would bring his favorite team good luck, or at least give them the edge in a tight situation.

As I felt the warmth of his hand, it seemed as if I had known Doug forever. From the time of our first meeting, he was like one of my own sons. His mother, Carol, had called me one day from South Carolina, her anxious, tired voice filled with gratitude. "Deanna, our little son, Doug, has been diagnosed with a malignant brain tumor," she said. "A friend gave me a tape of your music, and I can't tell you how much it has helped our family. I put the music on as soon as I get up in the morning, and somehow it helps me through the day. It has been a great help for Doug too. He especially likes the Peacebird song—he thinks it was written just for him. The next time you come to South Carolina to give a workshop, could you come to our town and visit Doug? It would mean so much to all of us."

It was an invitation I could not refuse. During my next visit to South Carolina I took a detour through Aiken, where I met the child who was to become not only a dear friend but also one of my finest teachers. He was a beautiful, fair-haired boy with wide blue eyes and a remarkable sense of humor. His turned-up nose displayed a smattering of freckles. His flashing smile totally captured my heart.

Doug was surrounded with a strong support system of parents, brothers, and sisters who were honest with him about every aspect of his illness. From the initial diagnosis of his cancer, he was told about medications and treatments and their results. His personal awareness of what was happening seemed to produce in him incredible maturity. His first concern was for the comfort of others who worried about how to respond to him.

One day, on the way to Aiken to visit Doug, I discovered a toy dog at the airport I knew he would love. Stuffed animals were some of his prized possessions. After greeting him at the airport, I tucked the dog into his arms, and he immediately named him Sparky. When we stopped at a Pizza Hut for lunch, he placed Sparky carefully beside his plate. Carol had just informed me that, after a long remission, Doug's tumor was growing again. My heart was so heavy that I could only sample my food. Doug's appetite wasn't much better. After eating only a little of his pizza, he said, "I can't eat any more, Deanna. I'm too full."

"Why don't you feed the rest of the pizza to Sparky?" I tried to speak lightly, to sound casual.

"I can't," Doug quipped. "He's already stuffed."

When I erupted into gales of laughter, Doug smiled. His mission had been accomplished. I was at ease, and so was he.

Many months of various treatments failed to eradicate the tumor that was taking away my little friend's life. His family took him to the Bahamas, praying that innovative treatments there would help, but the cancer continued to spread. Knowing that he might not have much time to live, we tried to provide him with rich travel experiences and new friends.

Often during our visits Doug would lie on a sofa while I sat nearby, playing and singing his favorite songs. One he liked best was a song I had written for him, titled "Little Doug, My Special Friend":

> One word from you and I forget
> The many troubles and the trials I have met.
> You touch my heart, you help me grow.
> Oh, little Doug, my special friend,
> I love you so.
>
> One smile from you . . . here comes the sun!
> We count the colors of the rainbow one by one.
> You take my hand, you see me through.
> I wish that I could see the world the way you do.
>
> Roger Staubach is your hero,
> Sister Megan you adore,
> And you love the songs I've written just for you.
> Rose and Peter take you swimming,
> And I know how much you love going fishing
> With your grandpa after school.
>
> You see the stars, you love the rain.
> You feel the joy, you know the pain.
> The summer skies, the leaves that fall,
> You see them all with open heart. You see them all.
>
> One hour with you and time stands still.
> We chase the butterflies through daisies on the hill.
> You give much more than you can know.
> Oh, little Doug, my special friend, I love you so!

During other visits, when Doug was not so ill, we stretched our horizons by traveling together. Sometimes he was accompanied by his sister, Megan, a gentle spirit with sunshine hair. She was his nurse as well as his best friend, giving him shots when necessary and providing much-needed moral and spiritual support.

Once we raced through Disneyland, encouraging Doug to use a wheelchair to conserve his energy. Another time we invited him to visit Utah to acquaint him with the rugged beauty of the mountains. Rock Canyon, near our home, was his favorite place. His face became wistful as he watched my sons scramble up the jagged rocks for a glimpse of Utah Valley, wishing he could go with them.

We also visited the Grand Canyon, one of nature's most colorful miracles. Doug was timid about going down onto the narrow trails, but he was not afraid to chase the skunks that frequented the yard around our cabin at midnight. Clutching flashlights, we dodged boulders and sagebrush for a glimpse of the scurrying black and white creatures. I was thankful for weeks afterward that we didn't catch one and become the recipients of its intolerable spray!

One of the motels on the rim of the canyon had a large swimming pool, filled to the brim with cold water. Sitting timidly on the edge, I didn't want to appear cowardly to Doug, so after a few minutes of painful adjustment, I endured the agony of submerging my feet and finally my ankles in the icy water. But I just couldn't see myself going any further and wondered how I could gracefully back out. Doug was standing above me, watching my slow, hesitant descent with amusement and some impatience. Suddenly he sparkled at the thought of a marvelous idea. "Deanna, let's stand up here together at this end of the pool, jump in, and race to the other side. The winner will get a prize!"

"Sure," I said haltingly. Then I jumped to my feet and stood tall beside the boy with the pale cheeks and scrawny legs. If he could do it, so could I.

"Ready, set, go!" Doug shouted with all the enthusiasm of a referee.

I plunged into the pool and felt myself being swallowed up by the cold liquid. I surfaced and began to swim as hard as I could to the other end. Since my swimming ability was limited, I didn't look back to pinpoint Doug's location. All I knew was that he was somewhere behind me and that I was cold enough to make as fast an exit from the pool as possible.

In the splash and gurgle of the churning water, I heard laughter ringing through the air. I glanced over my shoulder. Doug was standing bone dry on the edge of the pool, his slender form outlined against a white sun. "You did it!" he cheered, his voice bubbling with laughter. "You won! You get the prize!"

The "prize" was new respect for a child who had learned to laugh in the midst of pain and adversity, even though he had pulled quite a trick on me.

Now, an inadvertent shove from an overzealous Cowboys fan reminded me that we were in Dallas, ready to face another adventure. When we found our seats, Doug reached deep into his pocket and pulled out his two furry good-luck friends. With such support up in the bleachers, how could the Cowboys possibly lose? If I hadn't been a confirmed football fan before, I was now undeniably caught up in the spell of the game, along with about 63,000 other fans packed into Texas Stadium. Hospitals and radiation treatments were forgotten in the wonder and excitement of blue and white stars painted on a green field, shining under brilliant lights. If the Dallas Cowboys were going to win the NFC East Division Championship, they had to win this game.

There was a slight hush in the crowd, and then screams of approval as the players emerged from the other side of the field. Doug's eyes were fastened on one of the Cowboys, and he shouted, "Here he comes!" A special relationship had formed between Doug and player number 12. To Doug, Roger Staubach was not just the world's greatest quarterback. He was someone who cared deeply for a little child up in the stands, a friend who was pulling as hard for Doug as Doug was pulling for him. Roger was symbolic of a man who plunges into the game of life, who gives it and lives it his

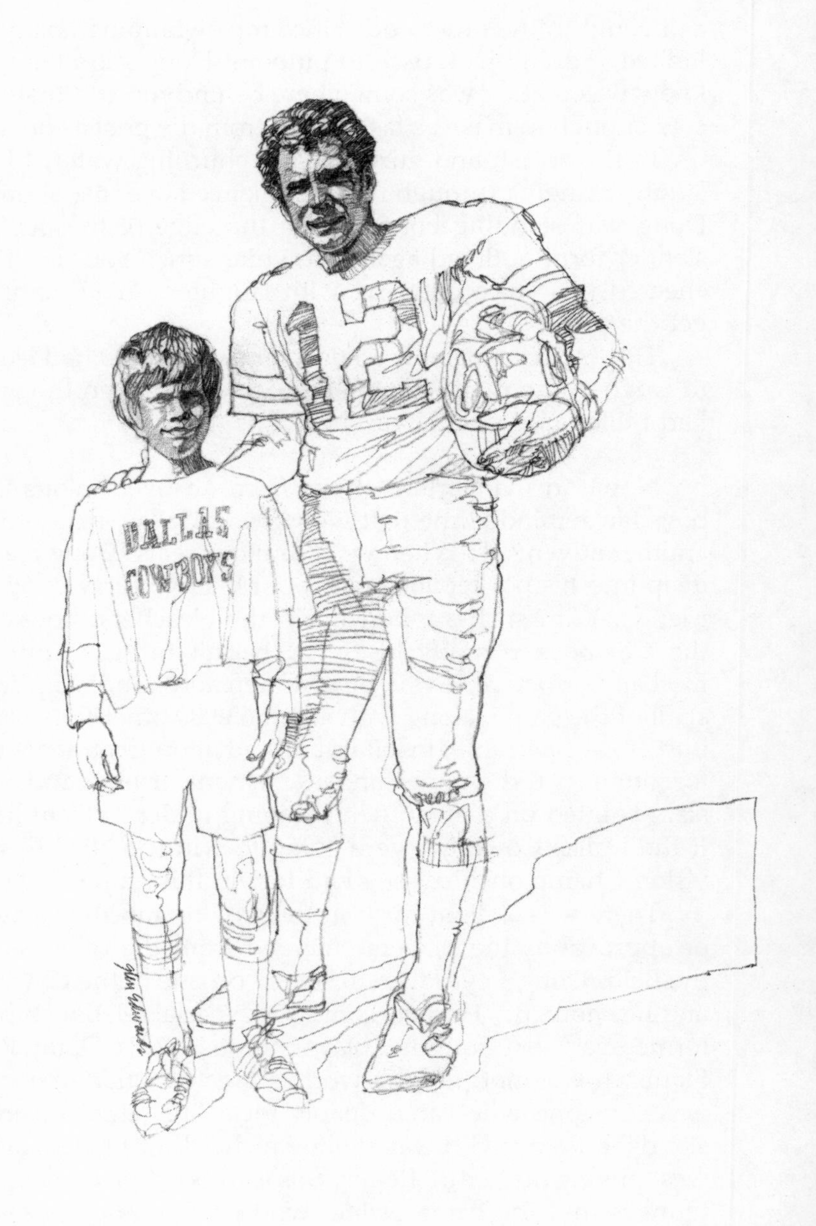
12
DALLAS
COWBOYS

best, even when he is hurting. Doug's love for Roger would transcend the icy weather and the roar of the fans cheering for victory.

Undistracted by spilled popcorn and noisy hotdog vendors, Steve and Doug watched the field intently. Today the Cowboys were playing against their longstanding rivals, the Washington Redskins. The Cowboys' strong defensive unit suffered as the Redskins pulled out ahead, 17 to 0, early in the game. By halftime the Cowboys were leading by three points. In the early minutes of the third quarter the Cowboys were ahead, and the fans screamed their approval. But their excitement was short-lived. The next twenty-five minutes seemed endless as disheartened Texans watched the Washington Redskins continue to score, including a 66-yard touchdown that brought the score to 34 to 21. With only five minutes left, the Cowboys appeared to be finished.

I glanced over at the boys. Lines wrinkled Steve's forehead as he watched the action on the field in silence. I was more concerned about Doug, however. He had come so far to watch the game, and I yearned for him to leave Dallas in high spirits.

People around us began to stir restlessly. About ten thousand fans picked up their coats and blankets and began to move toward the exits. But Doug was not about to give up. He squinted, then suddenly got to his feet, waving his furry seal and his rabbit's foot high in the air. The game was not over yet. Five minutes was still time enough for a miracle!

In an amazing turn of events, Randy White of the Cowboys recovered a Washington fumble. It took Staubach exactly three passes to get the Cowboys into the end zone to score a touchdown. Doug's eyes began to sparkle brighter than the lights around the field. "You did it, Roger!" he shouted.

With Dallas trailing by six points and less than four minutes left, both teams lined up for the kick-off. Dallas attempted an on-side kick, and the Redskins were unable to get possession of the ball. Now all eyes were on number 12 as the Cowboys moved down the field. The national television audience and the remaining fans could hardly believe their eyes when Roger Staubach threw another electrifying pass. Tony Hill hauled in the pass and stepped into the end zone for a touchdown with forty-two seconds left in the game. Now Doug's excitement could hardly be contained. The score was tied! Rafael Steptien ran onto the field, positioned himself, and kicked the extra point giving Dallas a 35 to 34 victory!

One second left in the game—one second to capture an eternal moment in the glorious smile on the face of a little boy—and then it was over. The stadium went wild in a marvelous kaleidoscope of sound and color. I hugged Steve, then picked up Doug and held him high in the air, burying my cold nose in his frosty cheek. "We won! We really did it! We won the game!"

"We are born to win," Doug said, smiling broadly.

Tears burned my eyes. That moment was an affirmation to Doug that faith and courage can make all the difference. Through long, agonizing days and months, through radiation and chemotherapy treatments, he had proven that he could pull off a victory during the final countdown, a victory of the spirit. For Roger Staubach, it was the most thrilling game of his career and the first time in history that the Cowboys had overcome a thirteen-point deficit in such a brief time.

Several months later, Doug was transferred to a hospital in Portland, Oregon. Remarkable new research was being done that soon would enable doctors to fight tumors, without further damaging the system, for patients who had already had as much chemotherapy as their bodies could tolerate. All of our hopes were raised, and we prayed that Doug would qualify for treatment.

After thorough testing, Doug's doctors decided that the tumor was too extensive, and they made the difficult decision to reject him for the experimental program. He was to be sent home without treatment. Armed with full knowledge of what was happening to him, and knowing he had little time left, Doug began to turn his attention to other critically ill children on the same unit.

One patient who particularly concerned Doug was Johnny, a boy near his own age. Curled in a fetal position on his bed in a darkened existence, Johnny waited for death to come. Like Doug, he had a brain tumor; but unlike Doug, he didn't have a strong system of love and support. His parents were divorced, and, to our knowledge, his father didn't come to visit him even once during his last stay in the hospital. His mother came only a few times before he died.

In such cases it is imperative that we refrain from being judgmental. Some parents, unable to watch their children die, say their final good-byes when the child enters the hospital. When the parents' wall of fear becomes too deep to penetrate, the hospital staff becomes the dying child's surrogate family. In Johnny's case, even the efforts of the staff were not enough. He refused to eat, to smile, or to speak with the nurses. No one seemed to be able to reach him.

Then one day Doug quietly entered Johnny's room. Afterwards there was a noticeable difference in Johnny's attitude. He began smiling again. He was hungry. He began talking with visitors.

After Doug returned to South Carolina, I went back to do a benefit concert for his family in the cathedral where Doug often served as the altar boy. Doug sat with his family near the front of the church. Suddenly a candy bar appeared, as if from nowhere. I almost laughed in the middle of a song when I saw Doug's careful attempts to remove the wrapper without being noticed. Finally he grabbed his coat and pulled it over his head so he could open and eat the candy in privacy.

Following the concert we spent some time together in Doug's grandmother's warm, sunny kitchen. Both he and I seemed to sense it would be our last meeting. We had shared so much, been through so much together. But "so much" is never enough when you have to say good-bye. I knew I could not leave Doug without knowing more about the secret conversation that had helped give Johnny, the child in Oregon, the will to live. I could not go until I was Doug's student one more time.

I placed my arm around his shoulders and put my face next to his. Decadron treatments had caused his face and cheeks to swell almost beyond recognition, but nothing had changed his enormous lashes and soft blue eyes. "Doug," I whispered, "before I go, I just want to know what you said to Johnny when you first visited him in the hospital. What did you say that made such a difference? I don't want to pry, but I think I can learn something from you about how to help other children like him."

Doug was modest as he reached back to recapture their conversation. "Oh, I didn't say much. I just told him I knew how he felt because I had a brain tumor just like his. I told him that if he had any unfinished business or work that he needed to do, I could help him do it." A mischievous smile crept over his face. "I told him the nurses didn't like it, but I had lots of candy bars hidden in my room, and I would share some with him whenever he got hungry."

The smile vanished as he searched for the rest of the conversation. "Oh yes, I told him that sometimes I felt like crying, and if he ever felt like crying, he could come into my room and we could cry together. The last thing I told him was, 'Don't be afraid to die, Johnny. I'm not afraid.' " Then he hesitated as he confessed, "To tell you the truth, Deanna, I am kinda scared, because I've never had any experience."

My breath caught in my throat. I held Doug close to me, awed by his wisdom and insight, and the gift of himself that he had so freely given to all of us. No psychiatrist on earth could have helped Johnny as well as Doug had helped him.

"Oh, I almost forgot," Doug said, pulling a piece of paper from his pocket. "Here is the poem I wrote for you."

I unfolded the paper and found a work of art that had taken him two and a half hours to create. In all my years of work, it was the finest compliment I had received. Through the tears in my eyes, I read:

> Deanna, my friend, so sweet and dear,
> She helps me to get by when I am in fear.
> When they are near there is no need to shed a tear

For there is no fear.
My sister, Megan, Deanna and I travel when we can.
We run through the grass and play in the sand—
Sing and rejoice and have fun again.
We travel over the mountains and across the land
Chasing skunks in the Grand Canyon.
In Utah we roast weenies around the campfire
And then we make smores and end up just wanting more.
When we have a chance, we go see our hero play.
He is the number one quarterback to us and there is no fuss.
He plays for the Cowboys and we win, win, win.
His name is Roger Staubach, and that is the end.

I was amazed that a little boy with only weeks to live was talking about singing, rejoicing, and having fun.

A few weeks later, with Christmas coming again, I hurried to the post office with a big box of presents I had picked out for Doug and his family. "Send it the fastest way you can," I said to the postmaster. "This will probably be my little friend's last Christmas, and I want to be sure he has a chance to open these gifts."

When I returned home, Cliff was standing at the door. He gathered me into his arms. "Honey, I hate to tell you this. Carol just called. Doug died this morning."

Even when a long-term illness has been with us an extended period of time, we are never prepared for that final parting. It always comes as a shock. The fragile mortality of those we love seems incomprehensible until their physical presence is no longer with us. Hot tears washed through me, and my first thought was painful. "But Doug won't get to open the presents I sent him," I said. My second thought, however, was as bright as the Star of Bethlehem. "Doug got the best Christmas present of us all—the Christ Himself."

I thought back to a time when Doug and I were sitting in an airport and Doug said, "I can't die, Deanna. Too many people love me."

I sighed, and for a moment I yearned to say, "Doug, why can't you bargain with God and come back to us?"

Doug's family invited me to conduct a memorial service the night before the funeral mass. It was to be a celebration of the life of the child who had taught us more than we could have learned in any classroom, a time to remember his joy and his love for life.

During my airplane flight to South Carolina, I thought of a note our friend Trina Paulus had written and sent to him: "There are always miracles, but the main miracle is our life and loving—bringing love from flower to flower. Whether your journey to God is long or short, what counts is getting there and loving as we go."

I wanted to reassure the family of the little boy who had loved God so well that he was in heaven with Him and that he was safe and happy. Parents often ask themselves when they lose a child, "Will I see my child again?" "Is my child in heaven?" "What is heaven like?" "What is my child doing right now?" "Was there someone to meet my child when he died?" "Is he well cared for by those who love him?"

Most families will do everything possible to find a missing child. When a child dies, family members feel many of the same emotions. They know they can't "find" the child as they could if the child had just run off and gotten lost. But they yearn for reassurance that they will be reunited some day. Many parents have said to me, "I pray that someone in heaven will love my child until I get there."

I smiled inwardly as I wondered if Doug would still be chasing skunks with flashlights in heaven. Surely he would be doing the same things there that he had enjoyed doing here. I couldn't envision heaven as a remote, fancy place with golden streets and marble palaces. Instead, I could see Doug probably turning everything upside down with his laughter and mischief. I took out my pen and notebook and wrote a last song for a child I thought must surely be the most special little angel in heaven at that moment:

The Littlest Angel

The littlest angel in heaven
Loves kittens and cowboys and fun.
Heaven will never be just as it was
Now that his life there's begun.

He'll turn fluffy clouds into snowmen
And swing on the stars up above.
He'll turn golden streets into playgrounds
And fill up God's home with his love.

He'll make dandelions out of sunbeams
And find grassy meadows for playing.
His laughter will ring where the great choirs sing,
But he'll hear me whenever I'm praying.

The littlest angel in heaven
Is one I am longing to see,
For the child that belongs now with Jesus
Is the child that belonged once with me.

9
Going Home

One spring, as we were beginning to plan our summer trip home, Cliff received a call from the Secondary Education Department at Brigham Young University in Provo, Utah. The department was interested in his teaching experience and his extensive publishing record in curriculum development and was inviting him to interview for a position on their staff. We were elated but tried to keep our hopes in perspective. Going home to Utah would mean closer association with family and friends and an opportunity to live near the mountains and help build the dream cabin that Cliff and his brother had been planning for years. Cliff flew to Utah for the interview, and several weeks later he was offered the position.

I soon realized that leaving Illinois would mean leaving my work and my friends at Mennonite Hospital. The patients I had met there would always fit solidly into my heart—Mr. Joy, Mrs. Outlaw, and Mr. Jones. Vickie Lannie and Sylvia Bellows, my singing partners, and so many others would remain in my memory. How could I ever forget pushing Sylvia's wheelchair through the snow over the Illinois State University campus or helping to lift her wheelchair up the flights of stairs so she could attend the music therapy classes?

I knew I would be moving away from direct access to a music-therapy department, but my own work had been moving another direction. The likelihood of my working as a registered music therapist on a daily basis in one facility began to fade when I started receiving more and more requests for workshops from all parts of the United States, Canada, and New Zealand. Calls were coming from long- and short-term care facilities, hospitals, nursing homes, and universities. I began to feel that if I could help to sensitize people in the health-care professions to the value of music as a therapy, they would be more open about hiring the growing number of registered therapists who were looking for permanent work.

Cliff and I were thrilled to call our parents and give them the good news. After ten years of separation, we were finally going home! I affectionately called my father-in-law "Dad" because he filled such a special place in my heart. He was unmistakably joyous at the news, but something in the sound of his voice disturbed me. "I haven't been feeling too well lately," he confided. "My stomach's been bothering me more and more."

My heart sank. We had been pleading with Dad for months to go to a doctor. Believing himself to be indestructible, he would never listen to us. "Oh, the doctor will just give me some anti-acid and send me home," he'd say. "Then he'll send me a bill. It would just be a waste of my time and his." Then he would silently continue to endure his discomfort. For Dad to even mention the word *pain,* it had to be serious.

"The doctor wants me in for gallbladder surgery," he added. "Guess I'll be going to the hospital soon."

His voice brightened when we talked about our plans for coming home and for leaving the boys with him and Mum for a few days while we scouted the Provo area for a home. As soon as spring semester was over, we would make our move and begin preparations for the fall semester at Brigham Young University.

"I'm so happy!" Dad said. "Now I'll get to see my grandsons more often, and Shon and I can go fishing this summer up on the Logan River."

The following afternoon when I walked into the house

with a bag of groceries, one of the boys handed me a note to call Jeanne Glynn, the talk-show hostess for the nationally syndicated television program *Christopher Closeup*. My second appearance with the Christophers had just aired nationally from New York to Los Angeles. A call from the Christophers usually meant a discussion about the mail response for my previous appearance, or the possibility of a new program in the future. It would give me an opportunity to tell Jeanne about our offer to teach in the West.

I called the New York office, and Cecilia Harriendorf, a good friend and the associate producer of the show, answered. "Jeanne is out of her office right now," she said, "but she asked me to give you some news that's not good. Deanna, I'm really sorry to have to be the one to tell you this, but Joan Paul was tragically killed here in New York. We tried but were unable to reach you before her funeral service, which was held a few days ago. Here at the studio we're still in a state of disbelief. She was not only a great leader in religious broadcasting but a dear friend as well. We at the Christophers are going to have a memorial service for Joan this week in New York. We've had several calls from people asking if you're going to be here. Joan loved you so much, and your music was so meaningful to her. Can you come and sing at the service?"

"Joan Paul is dead!" The words whirled in my mind, sending me into shock. Joan had swept into my life on autumn winds and filled an empty place with hope and love. When no one in the music industry believed or cared, Joan did. Whenever I needed to see a light in the darkness, her candle was there, smoldering at times and flaring brightly at others, but always there. Without her help, I might never have had the strength and the courage to climb the mountain. Joan had believed in me in a way that perhaps no would ever believe again. How I would miss her!

New York City, with its multitudes of people, was never a lonelier place than when I arrived the evening before the memorial service with the knowledge that Joan was no longer there. Through a sleepy haze the next morning, the sharp pain of grief drifted back into my awareness. Joan would not have wanted it to be a day just for tears, I reminded myself. Our best memorial would be a celebration. I could almost hear her saying, "Take your sadness, Deanna, and make something beautiful for God."

At the Christopher studio, Joan's television family, friends, and relatives met one another for the first time. We shared tears, joys, and memories. Many of us shared a few words during the memorial service about the individual roles Joan had played in our lives. Her picture was placed amidst yellow roses, and her presence was very much with us. Her delightful and subtle sense of humor was reflected in the comments made during the service.

The words I found especially comforting came from Joan's good friend, Father Charles Dolan, who had worked extensively with her on *Christian in Action, Guideline,* and other programs for the major networks. Their personal and professional rapport was warmly communicated by his timely message, from which I quote a few excerpts:

> Today represents the marvelous paradox of prayer. Prayer is a debt we owe to God—but when we pray, it's ourselves we pay. God doesn't need our prayers. We need them. No one could—and I know I can't—do justice to the person Joan was and the life she lived. It is a debt we owe to honor her memory. But in paying it, we are rewarded. She does not need our praise. Her accomplishments speak for themselves. We need the reminder and the inspiration of her deep and abiding faith, her strong and courageous hope, her all-encompassing love. . . .
>
> Joan's compassion and dedication to the poor and the sick of the world, individually and collectively, encompassed her, as she sheltered strays, both animal and human. There isn't one of us who isn't deeply in her debt just by having known her.
>
> A simple story consoles me. We've all sat on the lawn on a summer's evening with a group, in that exaggerated dark of an early summer's night. There's a light on in the

> house, and through the open door an avenue of light stabs across the darkened lawn. Somebody in the group gets up to go into the house. As she walks down that avenue of light, her shadow lengthens behind her. Those who are left on the lawn see only the lengthening shadow. There is something mysterious and sad about it. But the one who is walking into the house sees no shadow at all. It's all behind. All she sees is the light toward which she's walking until she is completely bathed in it. We are left on the darkened lawn of the world with the ache and shadow of her passing, but for her, Eternal Life.

I didn't realize it then, but Father Dolan's words were to be an added source of comfort in the weeks to come.

"We did it," Jeanne smiled after the service. "We just had a big, wonderful family reunion. I think Joan would have been very proud of us!"

Upon my return from New York, I heard the shattering news about Cliff's father. Dad had gone into the hospital for what we thought would be a simple gallbladder operation. But when the doctors operated, they found he was full of cancer, with most of his vital organs involved. His condition was inoperable. He had hardly been sick a day in his life, and now he was dying.

I cried through the night until I was exhausted. Losing two loved ones so close together was extremely difficult for me. Dad was the only grandfather our children had known. We had a new little son now, Eric, an adorable twenty-two-month-old with wide blue eyes and honey-blond hair. Grandpa had seen him only once, during our brief visit home the summer before. Our toughest question was how to tell Shon. Shon had a wealth of memories. The other boys were too young when we left Utah to have experienced all the good times Shon had enjoyed with Grandpa. It wasn't fair, I thought. But cancer is never "fair." Besides, if Dad lived through the summer, would he have to suffer through the incredible pain that so many cancer patients experience?

Once again I was at the crossroads. I could see my own father's face before me as if it were yesterday. Somewhere in the back of my mind, I could hear Dick Obershaw's words during our workshop in Richmond: "Deanna, someday another person may come into your life who needs you in the way your father needed you when he was dying. Do all the things for him that you never did for your father. Get involved. Be there. It will help to heal the hurt."

I determined that whatever Dad had to go through, he would not have to go through it alone. With shaking hands I dialed the hospital number. According to Cliff, Dad had just been told the news about his condition. I would let him know that I knew from the beginning. Even if it was long distance, we would see it through together.

Suddenly, Dad's voice was on the other end. He sounded weak, tired, and frightened.

"How are you feeling, Dad?" I asked. The words stuck like straw in my throat, and I knew I should not have said them. He had just been told he had cancer, and I was asking how he was feeling!

"I'm fine," he said. "Doing just fine."

Where had I heard that it is extremely difficult to be objective when members of your own family are critically ill? It would not be the last time I would falter in my communication with Dad. I would just have to try it again.

"Dad, I know about the cancer. I know it's bad."

I heard a sob on the other end of the line, and I could feel him close to me as I spiritually hugged him. All the miles between us seemed to disappear in that brief silence as we shared the pain.

"I love you, Dad, more than I can say."

"I love all of you so much! Sorry this had to happen as you were coming home. The doctor says I won't have to spend the rest of my time in the hospital. He says I can go home as soon as I can keep a little food down. I may even be able to go back to work for a while."

His hope was contagious, and I allowed myself to be

touched by it. "We'll be there soon, Dad," I said. "Just hang on for us. We'll be with you all the way, in every thought and prayer. Dad, if you ever feel like talking, remember I'm here."

Cliff and I talked with the boys when they returned home from school. I gathered Shon into my arms. It seemed just yesterday that he was only eight pounds, tiny enough to fit into one of Mum's dresser drawers when we visited her and Dad. When Shon was fussy, Dad would lay him across his chest, rub his back, and sing "That Little Boy of Mine." The news of Dad's illness would not be easy for Shon.

I was as gentle as I could be. "Honey, we just received the news that Grandpa is very ill," I explained. "He has cancer, a disease that has spread so far through his body that the doctors can't stop it from growing. It's so serious, he may not have very long to live. So right now we have to give him the very best love we can for as long as we can. We know how close you are to Grandpa, and we know this will be especially hard for you."

The disbelief in Shon's eyes blocked the tears that were trying to form, tears I knew would come later. He stayed in his bedroom for a long time, composing a letter to Grandpa to tell him all the things that needed to be said.

I still had a few workshops to complete before our trip to Utah. In order to establish priorities, I had been accepting programs only in the spring and fall months so I could be home fulltime with the family at least six to seven months of the year.

I had been asked to give a seminar for health-care professionals in Waycross, Georgia, a small southern town near the border of Florida. As I was preparing my lecture in my hotel room in Georgia, another call came from Cliff. Dad's condition was much worse. He had almost died the night before, and the entire family was being notified. We decided Cliff should start out with the boys by car, and I would fly to Utah to try to get there before Dad died.

I cut short my workshop schedule in Waycross and immediately called to make an airline reservation to Salt Lake City. The wait on the line was interminable. One of the airlines was on strike, and operators were having difficulty answering the volume of calls coming in. Finally I reached the reservations department, and learned that air service in the smaller southern towns was extremely limited. I would have to leave in the middle of the night and would have to stop in four states to reach Utah.

Never has a night been so long as that night. The wait between flights seemed endless. I had the feeling that Dad would wait for me if I hurried fast enough. I just had to say "I love you" one more time.

Once in Salt Lake City, I borrowed my sister's car. Though I was exhausted and numb, the memories kept me going. Cliff and I had hoped to come back home and find everything just as it was when we left it ten years earlier: the fresh aroma of roast beef in the oven, the hunting and fishing with Dad, and the late night visits around the kitchen table. I could still hear Dad's hearty, rich voice singing his own special version of "The Old Gray Mare" and see his reluctant smile when he had to be coaxed to sing it at family reunions. Dad was a great man, quiet and loving, strong, yet vulnerable. He loved so many people. And they loved him. He was only sixty-two years old. Why him? Why now?

When I arrived at the hospital, I was told that Cliff's father had died several hours earlier. I let the tears come as I left. In a few minutes I was with the family gathered together in the little house by the river that Mum and Dad had shared for so long. We sat in the living room and went over and over the details of Dad's illness and death. I wanted to know everything, to share vicariously the last weeks of his mortal life.

As I plunged headlong into the grief work, a work I had been so reluctant to do for my own father, I was reminded of Father Dolan's words: "Goodness is all but taken for granted in the gradual day, but in the light of eternity we can see how blessed we have been." How blessed we had been to have had both Dad and Joan among us!

I was grateful that Cliff had enjoyed such a good visit with Dad during his trip to Utah for the job interview only weeks before. Telling the boys would be the hardest part, but I knew they needed to be an important part of the farewells to their grandfather.

After tracing and retracing the steps Dad had taken during his illness, we all went to the funeral home to make final arrangements. In the midst of all the necessary decisions, one thought was uppermost in my mind. I wanted to *feel* this experience.

This time I allowed myself to feel the pain and to be touched by it and taught by it. I had come full circle. This was my father-in-law, but in a special way it was also my own father. When Cliff's brother Glen asked me to sing at the funeral service, I hesitated only for a moment. "I'll break down," I said. "I'll cry in the middle of the song."

Glen wisely asked, "Can you think of anyone else Dad would rather have sing in your place?"

"I'll sing," I said quickly, all hesitation gone.

It was a simple but powerful farewell. In the few words I spoke before my song, I shared an intimate portrait of my father-in-law. I found in myself a strength I didn't know was there—truly the light within, the Holy Spirit. I wondered how many people had deprived themselves of an opportunity to participate in a funeral service because they had convinced themselves they were not strong enough.

I had written the song I sang especially for Dad while the memory of Joan's words were still in my heart: "Deanna, take your sadness and make something beautiful for God." I was not only learning to do grief work, I was also learning to create with it. It was a song of celebration, a song of warm remembering, a song of "going home."

Dad, you gave us so much
We can be thankful for.
By your faith you've shown us all
That love is an open door.
You lit so many candles
That we all could feel the glow,
And now it's hard, so very hard,
To let you go.

Dad, I guess you know
The way will be lonely now,

But you taught us, by the way you lived,
That life can be only now.
Today is all we have,
We can't see around the bend,
But we are glad—so very glad—
There is no end.

Going home, going home
To the arms of love.
You've seen His face, you have a place,
Now you're with God above.
And with all His warmth around you,
You will never be alone.
The pain is gone, and life goes on.
You're going home!

10

Remember Me

I settled back in my comfortable seat on the train, cradled my head against the headrest, and breathed a sigh of relief. My son Shon and I had just left the beautiful countries of Norway and Denmark and were on our way to Germany. Since Shon spoke fluent German, I was counting on him to be my guide and interpreter. Somehow my son and I had known that the last part of our European visit would be the most special. For eleven memorable days we would escape hotel rooms and train stations while getting to know and cherish the hearts and feelings of a German family who had been waiting for our arrival.

I glanced at Shon, whose head was buried in a travel guide, and then gazed out the window. Pools of sun falling through the clouds in patterns on the trees reminded me of a photograph that had been haunting me for months. It was a picture of a lovely young girl with full lips and large wistful eyes. Her long, wavy hair, crowned with sunlight from behind her, stood out vividly against the glistening leaves of a large tree.

I had first seen the photograph in Eau Claire, Wisconsin, at Sacred Heart Hospital. Two years earlier I had been invited to give a workshop for nurses and staff members at the hospital. I was pleasantly surprised by a last-minute invitation to give an after-dinner speech for a group of Wisconsin physicians the night before. It was a rare opportunity, and I quickly accepted.

Following the dinner and program, Dr. Chaudri shook my hand warmly. "I think music therapy offers the most help for treatment I've seen since the advent of antibiotics," he said, smiling. Then his face grew serious. "I have a young patient in the intensive-care unit at Sacred Heart Hospital. Her name is Astrid Müller. She's a seventeen-year-old foreign-exchange student from Germany who was involved in a bad traffic accident when a truck hit her side of the car. She's suffered massive brain injury. But there is always an outside chance that patients like her can hear or sense the presence of loved ones nearby. Her parents just arrived from Germany, and they're hurting deeply. I'd appreciate it if you'd meet with them after your workshop tomorrow. Perhaps you could sing to Astrid in the intensive-care unit. I believe your visit would mean a great deal to them."

That was one of those times when I wished the special assignment had been given to someone else. I shuddered to think how devastated these parents must be. I didn't know if they could speak English or would even understand why I had come to see them. But I told Dr. Chaudri I would be happy to visit with the family and that I would let him know of their response.

The following day as I gave the workshop, thoughts of the Müller family crept into my mind. What could I possibly say or do that would help to heal the hurt? After the program was over, I prayed for guidance and then set off with my escort to find the Müllers.

The couple from Germany were sitting in a small waiting room next to intensive care. When I was introduced to Gunther and Elke Müller, I was immediately impressed by an aura of love that seemed to surround both of them. Gunther's keen eyes, a piercing green, revealed rare sensitivity. Elke's eyes mirrored a great depth of suffering. This strikingly handsome couple appeared to have shared a lifetime of closeness.

Gunther was a grade-school principal and a teacher of

music, and when he saw my guitar, he seemed to understand why I had come. The unusual thing about the meeting was the way they made me feel loved and accepted. They were very solicitous and caring. It was as if they were making me feel at home rather than I them.

After embracing me, they invited me to sit down with them. "We're grateful that you have come," Gunther said. "We appreciate your interest in our beloved daughter, Astrid. We have two other daughters at home, but they were not able to come with us. Music has always been an important part of our family, and our prayer is that Astrid will be able to hear the songs we sing to her. Before we go into the intensive-care unit, we want to show you something."

He took a picture from an envelope and handed it to me. I looked for a long time at the photo of Astrid. A smile danced on her face, and her dark eyes sparkled with the hope of a thousand tomorrows. "Before we go in to sing at her bedside," Elke repeated softly, "we wanted you to see our daughter."

I understood what they were trying to say to me. Instead of the Astrid lying in a strange bed, her sparkling eyes taped shut, her luxurious brown hair wrapped in bandages, they wanted me to have a vision of the vibrant young girl I was singing to. It was a picture I would never forget.

We stood around her bed and sang songs to her in both German and English, hopeful that Astrid somehow would be able to hear the music and sense our love. I had learned to sing in sixteen languages as a teenager and found the songs to be helpful tools in my music therapy work. We tried to sing close to her ear and spoke intimate messages of hope and comfort.

It had been difficult for me to meet the Müller family, but it was far more difficult to say good-bye to them. In just moments, friendship had bonded us together, and I had been touched in a way I could not explain. The people I laugh with I may not always remember, but I seldom forget the people I cry with. Sharing deep moments of sorrow can create unbreakable bonds of trust.

Before leaving Wisconsin, I stopped at a gift shop to buy a miniature music box that had caught my eye. It was shaped like a book, and on the cover was a fully opened red rose. I lifted the lid to hear the charming, clear tones of "Love Makes the World Go Round." I took it to the hospital and asked a staff member to give it to Gunther and Elke so they could place it by Astrid's pillow and play it for her every day.

After I returned home, I kept in touch with the intensive-care unit by phone. One afternoon I learned that Astrid had died. There would be a brief memorial service in Wisconsin, and then her body would be flown back to Germany for burial. A priest who worked at the hospital, Father David Brehm, later told me Astrid had quietly slipped away as her father held her and sang to her Brahms' "Lullaby." Before going on to my next workshops, I had my own grieving to do.

A few weeks later I wrote to the Müller family, sharing with them my conviction that families are forever and that one day they would surely be reunited with their beautiful daughter. We kept in touch over the months and the miles and nourished the hope that one day we would meet again.

The train gradually slowed to a stop, and a sign appeared outside the little depot: Bad Zwischenahn. We had finally arrived in the tiny village near the North Sea in northwestern Germany.

Shon and I tugged our suitcases from the top rack and hauled them off the train. When we looked up, Gunther and Elke were striding toward us, in company with a sparkling, golden-haired daughter and a pudgy dog named Bobby. Gunther's warm greeting and hearty laughter revealed a warm sense of humor I had not witnessed during our somber moments together in Wisconsin. Christiane, the Müllers' daughter, was both shy and captivating. Her mastery of English was considerably less than her parents', but her smile communicated her desire to make new friends. She and Shon fell into a comfortable German dialogue while we loaded suitcases into the station wagon.

"I don't say everything in a correct way in English, but I try," Gunther said, smiling.

"The important thing is to communicate, not to speak with perfect English," I reassured him.

The Müllers' well-groomed dog, its coat golden brown and its eyes sad, jumped in with the luggage. Then we piled into the station wagon and drove down flower-lined boulevards to Hermann-Allmers-Weg 13, the Müllers' street. What had been just an address on a letter came alive as we arrived at their large, white brick residence half-hidden by trees.

The family had prepared Astrid's room for me. I could feel her presence in the sunny bedroom with orange closets and slanted ceiling. A fluffy, blue-flowered comforter was on the bed, and dolls decorated a shelf above a school desk. I was deeply moved.

After bringing our suitcases to us, Gunther and Elke showed us through the house, which Gunther had designed and built. In the dining room I noticed three pictures on the wall. On top was a picture of Petra, the Müllers' oldest daughter, who had been away at school and would be coming by train the following day. The bottom picture was of Christiane. In the middle was a picture of Astrid. The same unique wave inherited from her mother swept across her forehead, and her full lips were parted in a half-smile. But it was her dark eyes that dominated the picture. "That is my favorite picture of Astrid," said Gunther. "I took it shortly before she left for the United States."

Hanging in the dining room and living room were prize-winning pictures Astrid had drawn of Christiane and her father. The resemblance of father and daughter was unmistakable, revealing Astrid's unusually fine artistic talent.

As we passed the china cabinet, Elke paused and slid open the glass doors. "Several weeks after Astrid's funeral, a box arrived in the mail," she said in a low voice, pointing to the lower shelf and a scene of the nativity. Each figure had been meticulously and artfully painted. Even the shadows in the crevices had been painted into the folds of the clothing that Joseph, Mary, and the shepherds wore. The figurines had been completed by Astrid in the United States prior to her death, except for the baby Jesus. The thoughtful friend who had sent them to Elke and Gunther had painted the baby Jesus herself.

"We were shocked to receive it, and we cried for a long time, but it is very precious to us," said Elke.

"Music was also very important to Astrid," Gunther added, gesturing toward the piano that stood in a corner of the room. "She had a special love for classical music, and sometimes she and I would play duets on the organ and the piano."

In the master bedroom, on the headboard shelf above the bed, a familiar red rose caught my eye. It was the little music box I had give to the Müllers to play for Astrid. Elke picked it up, and the clear, bell-like tones tumbled out. "Love Makes the World Go Round." Our eyes reddened as the memory flooded our minds.

"We're glad that you were there," Elke said, "even though it was a terribly sad time for us."

"Yes," affirmed Gunther. "We've been waiting for someone we can talk to about Astrid. In Germany, death is a difficult subject for people to talk about, so often they say nothing at all. Those who do talk to us usually say, 'How terrible to lose your daughter in a foreign country!' But if Astrid had to leave us, we're grateful it could be in a place where we were surrounded with such great love. We had unlimited visiting privileges and were allowed to be constantly at her side in the intensive-care unit. We're not sure that could have happened in Germany.

"Alice Spanel, the woman who worked with the foreign-student exchange program, gave us her home so we wouldn't have to be in a strange motel. The day Astrid died, a woman came running out of her house nearby and threw her arms around me and kissed me. 'We're so sorry you have lost your beautiful daughter,' she said. I was a stranger to her, but she cared enough to share our sorrow. Even though it has been two years, we still have a great need to have Astrid live in our hearts, our thoughts, and our conversations, but many people are afraid to even say her name. So we're glad you have come."

Countless times I had stressed in my workshops the need people have to remember and to talk about a deceased loved one, and the deep need the living have to feel they will be remembered after death. My awareness was much greater now that I was sharing the Müllers' need to remember Astrid.

We walked from the bedroom out onto a patio that looked

as if it had been lifted from the pages of a magazine. Red and white geraniums stood in planters on a brown wooden fence separating an enclosed eating area from the wide, grassy backyard. Along the brick wall on one side of the patio, hanging plants and vines decorated the garden in bright shades of red and green. Gunther pointed out the tree Astrid had been standing near when he took the picture I had first seen of her. Elke handed me a copy of the picture, which had become her favorite.

"We want you to have this," she said.

After a light supper, the Müllers took Shon and me on a tour of their village. What I had imagined from gazing at a dot on the map could not compare with the fairy-tale-like beauty of Bad Zwischenahn. We drove past quaint gingerbread houses that appeared to have been taken from the pages of "Hansel and Gretel" and painted on the landscape. My heart danced with excitement as we drove close to a windmill near the edge of the lake.

"I've never seen a real windmill up close!" I exclaimed. "Do you suppose I could fit it into my suitcase when we go home?"

Inside the windmill gift shop, Gunther said, "You can't take the windmill, but you can take a picture of it." He showed us a postcard of the windmill with a group of carefree young folk dancers whirling on the grass, and pointed to the dark-haired beauty in the second row. "This is a picture of Astrid," he said. "This postcard was made before she left Germany." I purchased several so I could send them to Alice, Father David, and Dr. Chaudri.

Next we drove toward a church that was eight hundred years old. We walked through its meticulous grounds, and I became entranced by what appeared to be a cemetery, though it was very different from those I had seen in the United States. The yard was a patchwork quilt of miniature gardens, surrounded by square concrete borders, with pathways leading between gravesites. A new awareness flooded over me: though the German people were reticent to acknowledge death verbally, they found a nonverbal way to make up for it by pouring their love into these little pieces of earth. Gunther and Elke picked up small rakes and watering cans provided by the caretakers. They filled the cans at a water faucet and then led me to Astrid's private garden. They seemed to be in another world there, carefully raking away old, dried leaves and watering the flowers blooming in rainbow colors in front of the headstone. They discarded wilted blossoms and then rearranged fresh flowers in small vases. They cared for these flowers and shrubs as carefully as they had tended and nourished Astrid.

Above the grave, a tall headstone of red granite registered Astrid's birth and death dates. "We imported the headstone from an area in France where we used to go camping together," Gunther said.

"We don't go there anymore," Elke added. "There are still too many painful memories for us. Sometimes when I come here, I speak out loud to Astrid. It helps me to feel closer to her."

Gunther looked thoughtfully at the grave and said, "Her death has brought many changes in our lives. Material things don't seem to matter anymore. I had been drifting in my faith, but now we're closer to God, and we speak our love more to each other. We're still searching for answers and studying books to find comfort. But we realize that love is the only thing on earth we can give and take in such hard times. Love is something that comes directly from God and helps us to live and maybe to understand.

"We experienced this love in Wisconsin, and it brought us back to a life with God and to a life with future. The Bible is teaching us—and also medical persons tell us—of those who have died and come back to life and have seen a brilliant light and experienced a feeling of great joy. So now we believe that we need not be sad about our daughter. We have to learn to live without her, and we have to learn to live so we always can follow her, but we feel she is close to us. Living without our beloved child is very hard, and the most painful thing. But it comforts us to know we gave Astrid all our love, that she was happy in her short life, and that she is with God now."

Evening was falling, so we returned to the Müllers' home and settled in their living room. Here they shared with me their long, slow struggle back to some sense of normalcy following Astrid's death. Gunther had become more aggressive in his grief work, whereas Elke had become more reticent. Haunted by vivid dreams of Astrid, she had become somewhat reclusive, finding in the safety of home the security she yearned for. Gunther, however, wanted to reach out more and to discover and explore all his hidden fears and feelings.

"I want to go back to Wisconsin," he said, "back to all the places Astrid knew and loved before her death. I want to feel and be a part of every aspect of her life that I may have missed while she was away from us."

Elke shook her head. "I don't think I can ever go back to the United States or to the places Astrid visited there. It's still too painful for me. I still can't bring myself to face it all, or watch the home movies we made during our camping trips or listen to the tapes of Astrid when she was a little girl. I am still afraid to remember."

I went to my room briefly to retrieve some lecture notes from my suitcase. I had given a workshop in Boston for the New England Hospital Assembly shortly before we came to Europe, and I still had my notes. Once when I was teaching for the Beaverton School District in Oregon, I had discovered an essay on an office wall and made a copy of it. I handed the essay to Elke. "This is for you," I said. She scanned the page and nodded as she read the words:

> To laugh is to risk appearing the fool.
> To weep is to risk appearing sentimental.
> To reach out for another is to risk involvement.
> To expose feelings is to risk exposing your true self.
> To place your ideas, your dreams, before the crowd is to risk their loss.
> To love is to risk not being loved in return.

> To live is to risk dying.
> To hope is to risk despair.
> To try is to risk failure.
> But risks must be taken because the greatest hazard in life is to risk nothing. The person who risks nothing does nothing, has nothing, and is nothing. He may avoid suffering and sorrow but he simply cannot learn, feel, change, grow, love, live. Chained by his certitudes, he is a slave. He has forfeited freedom. Only a person who risks is free.

"When the time comes that you can return to the United States, go first to Wisconsin," I challenged gently. "Do the grief work you must do. Celebrate Astrid's life. Enjoy renewing friendships. Then come to Utah and spend a few weeks with us. We have some of the most beautiful scenery in the world. We'd be honored to have you with us and show you our canyons and our national parks. Going back will hurt deeply. But as you take the risks, there'll come a healing and a peace that you have not known in a very long time."

The days to follow were a happy kaleidoscope of activities. We laughed, danced, sang, and cried together. Elke said that we would all have *breiten mund* (a bright mouth) when it was time to say good-bye. We had all laughed so hard, she said, that we would not be able to take our smiles off, and we would all look like grinning pumpkins.

I was getting to know Astrid better because of the goodness and greatness of her parents.

One evening Gunther suggested that we look at some old family movies. I knew it would be difficult for Elke to see films of her daughter for the first time since her death, so I whispered "I'll be here" to her while Gunther set up the screen and projector. I was very proud of her as I watched her risk the pain so that I could share the memories of Astrid splashing in the waves and running on the beach with her sisters, her brown hair flying in the wind, her smooth skin browned by the sun. It made me feel as if I had met Astrid before.

"I wish you could have known her," Elke whispered. "She was such a sunshine."

We also listened to tapes of the girls singing when they were small. Their childlike voices spilled into the room as if it were yesterday.

The following day we visited the little church where Astrid and Gunther had played the organ on special Sundays.

When we arrived home, Elke and Gunther prepared supper while I sat in the silence of Astrid's room. In an inexplicable way, I sensed her presence. I had been wanting to write a song especially for her, and now that I had seen the places she had known and loved, it seemed the perfect time to write.

"What would you have me say of you?" I asked Astrid silently.

The impression was simple and direct: "Tell them not to be afraid to remember me. Soon we will meet again. Until then, the only way we can communicate is through the power of love. When they feel love growing in their hearts, I will be there."

I picked up a pen and wrote a song for Astrid.

> Remember me whenever you see a sunrise.
> Remember me whenever you see a star.
> Remember me whenever you see a rainbow
> Or woods in autumn colors from afar.
>
> Remember me whenever you see the roses
> Or seagulls sailing high in a sky of blue.
> Remember me whenever you see waves
> shining in the sun.
> And remember, I'll be remembering you!
>
> Remember me whenever you see a teardrop
> Or meadows still wet with the morning
> dew.
> Remember me whenever you feel love
> growing in your heart.
> And remember, I'll be remembering you!

I hurried downstairs and called the Müllers from the

kitchen. Gunther stood behind me and Elke snuggled into the sofa as I sang Astrid's song for the first time. My fingers flew comfortably over the piano keys in an arrangement I felt I had been playing for years. It was a time for us to smile through our tears, with a song that would help everyone remember Astrid without fear or pain. It was a song we were to sing often in the short remaining days in Bad Zwischenahn.

Before our visit was over, the Müllers and I had an opportunity to do some music therapy work at Bethel, a large clinic for epileptics that is run by the Lutheran church. Bethel, which is located in the city of Bielefield, is actually a city within a city, with its own post office, currency exchange, shops, and grocery stores.

We went first to the main clinic, where murals created by the residents represent the Ten Commandments. I was impressed with how much of the interior decoration had been created by the patients and residents at Bethel, including a wide variety of crafts available in the gift shops.

After viewing the murals, we went to the home of Gunther's Aunt Maria, who, with her husband, Alfred, lives in a huge gray stone house in Bethel. Maria, an efficient, warm woman with a ready smile, works in the bookstore, while Alfred is a chaplain at Bethel.

After serving us a delicious lunch, Maria joined us in a sing-along around her piano. She, too, loved the song I had written for Astrid. Then she gave us a more extensive tour of the grounds and escorted us to the activity section of the facility. The rooms were divided into sections for various arts and crafts. I was amazed at the residents. All were seated and waiting when Shon and I arrived with Elke and Maria. Maria, who served as our translator, explained the songs and stories that I shared in English. Shon, in his deep bass voice, joined me. At the end of the program we began to sing a lively German song. Suddenly harmonicas mysteriously appeared, and the residents began to play in perfect harmony and rhythm to the music. Then the music director passed out other instruments, and they surprised me with a program of German songs they had prepared just for Shon and me. They also presented us with a copy of a book containing all the songs they had played for us. We were very moved. They said they would always remember our visit, and we spoke with as many individuals as we could.

Before leaving Bielefeld, we dropped Christiane off at Petra's dormitory. We felt that the best way to say good-bye was with a song, so we all stood out on the street together and sang "Love is something if you give it away." Petra, her friend Hubertus, and Christiane were still singing when we pulled away and began the long drive back to Bad Zwischenahn.

The emotional freedom, the open conversations about Astrid, the grief work, the sightseeing—and the music, laughter, and tears—had been good for all of us. It would be so hard to say good-bye. But there was another meeting to look forward to.

"We'll try to come to America next summer, spend some time in Wisconsin, and then come and visit you in Utah," Gunther promised.

He didn't know it at the time, but I was already planning a memorial concert for Astrid in Eau Claire. I knew that Father David and our friends at Sacred Heart Hospital would help.

Before we left the house, I quietly crept back into the living room and left a note on the table for Gunther and Elke to read after we had gone. I had written it the night before, as a reminder for them to keep us in their hearts. It ended with these words: "When one door closes, God always opens another, but we often look so longingly at the door that has closed that we fail to see the light shining from the door that has opened before us. As you look toward that light, do not be as concerned with written words that fall upon the eyes or spoken words that touch the ears. Like the distant sound of the coo-coo bird in the hushed stillness of the evening forest, be aware of what falls softly upon your hearts. It is the power of love. You will know it when it comes to you and gives your spirit wings!"

Through the years of my work, I learned a powerful truth that was beautifully summarized by Sam Keen when he said, "Intimacy is both terrifying and wonderful because it shatters our safe boundaries and polished self-images. When we touch and allow ourselves to be touched, we are enlarged and changed by the contact. True intimacy comes only after we discover that we can never take away each other's loneliness, fill the void in the bottom of the heart, make the world safe, banish tragedy, or take away the shadow of death. In the end, the best we can do is hold each other in this luminous darkness. And if, through our struggles, we finally come to be close to each other, that is enough."

I had learned to face my own fears and feelings, to communicate more openly and honestly, to physically touch the wounded with a gentle and tender hand, to listen with a sense of leisure, and to follow up when there had been an accident, illness, or injury. Most of all, I had learned the vital importance of loving and coming close to others. We cannot answer all the questions that appear in the presence of loss, but we can love deeply, and love itself brings healing.

For a song that became a therapy, even for me, I wrote these words:

I can't remove your loneliness or heal your broken heart,
Can't take away the shadows that make your life so dark,
But I can stay beside you when life is getting tough,
And if we come close together, that's enough.

I don't have all the answers, and I don't know what to say;
I can't bring you the sunshine or take the rain away;
But I can always hold you when the storm is getting rough,
And if we come close together, that's enough.

I had to learn so many things and fail so many times
Before the day I finally realized
If we could take the sorrow from every loss that comes along,
We'd have to take the loving out of life!

Music Brings My Heart Back Home

I can't remove the dangers from a world so full of fears;
I can't make living safer or take away your tears;
But I can always love you with a love that you can trust,
And if we come close together, that's enough!

Indeed, if we all come close together, that's enough!

Index

Index

Index

About the Author

Deanna Edwards has recorded six albums and, in addition to writing books, has been a contributing author for the book *Nursing Care of Children and Families: A Holistic Approach* (Addison Wesley Publishing Co.). For three years she served on the foundation board of directors for the American College of Health Care Administrators. Among the honors she has received are the following: Outstanding Young Woman of the Year for the state of Utah, 1978; Distinguished Service to Mankind Award, presented by the Orem, Utah, chapter of Sertoma International, 1983; and one of fifty American heroines featured in *Ladies' Home Journal,* July 1984. Articles about her work have appeared in *Ladies' Home Journal, Ladies Circle,* and *The American Health Care Association Journal,* and many newspapers. She has studied education and music therapy at Utah State University and Illinois State University, and uses music in teaching and therapy as well as to entertain.